Webb
Photo Phonology

Minimal Pair Cards
Fun Sheets

Written by Ashley Drennan
Photography by Sharon G. Webber
Edited by Lisa Priddy

www.superduperinc.com • Email: customerhelp@superduperinc.com
Post Office Box 24997, Greenville, South Carolina 29616
Call 1-800-277-8737 • Fax 1-800-978-7379

ISBN 1-58650-488-6

Super Duper® Publications

Introduction

Webber® Photo Phonology Minimal Pair Cards Fun Sheets is the perfect complement to the *Webber® Photo Phonology Minimal Pair Cards*. Like the photo cards, this workbook targets 10 phonological processes: *Final Consonant Deletion, Fronting, Stopping, Cluster Reduction, Stridency Deletion, Gliding, Prevocalic Voicing, Postvocalic Devoicing, Initial Consonant Deletion,* and *Nasalization.* Each section of the book reviews a phonological process and teaches all 28 pairs of photo cards found in each deck.

Although the worksheets vary, the activities in each section are the same. They will help your students develop discrimination and listening skills first, and then move to the production of target sounds at the word, phrase, and sentence level. The worksheets also improve vocabulary and grammar skills. The sections are organized and meant to be taught in the following order:

1. Auditory Bombardment- each section contains 100 target words to read aloud to your students to improve sound awareness skills.

2. Minimal Contrast Pairs- minimal pairs (tea/key) provide an opportunity to improve your students' auditory discrimination skills.

3. Minimal Contrast Pair Definitions- minimal pair definitions improve students' understanding of word meanings.

4. Word activities

5. Phrase activities

6. Sentence activities

You can use the activity sheets in therapy or for homework. The activity pages work best with children ages three and up. As they complete each motivating activity, your students will learn to accurately produce their target sounds. The workbook also contains a parent letter, two different tracking forms, and award certificates. A CD-ROM with the same black and white pages as the book is also included.

Table of Contents

#BK-320 Webber® Photo Phonology Minimal Pair Cards Fun Sheets • ©2005 Super Duper® Publications • www.superduperinc.com • 1-800-277-8737

Table of Contents

Parent/Helper Letter

Date: _____

Dear Parent/Helper:

Your child is currently working on _____ in Speech and Language Class.

The attached worksheet(s) will help your child practice and reinforce skills reviewed in the classroom.

☐ Please complete these activities with your child and return them signed by _____.

☐ Please complete these activities with your child. You do not need to return them to me.

☐ _____

_____

_____

Thank you for your support.

_____   _____
Name   Parent/Helper's Signature

#BK-320 Webber® Photo Phonology Minimal Pair Cards Fun Sheets • ©2005 Super Duper® Publications • www.superduperinc.com • 1-800-277-8737

Tracking Sheet

Name _____   Date _____

_____
Phonological Process

Correct Responses/Total Percentage

_____
Word/Phrase/Sentence Level

☐ ☐ ☐ ☐ ☐ ☐ ☐ ☐ ☐ = ____%

Name _____   Date _____

_____
Phonological Process

Correct Responses/Total Percentage

_____
Word/Phrase/Sentence Level

☐ ☐ ☐ ☐ ☐ ☐ ☐ ☐ ☐ = ____%

Name _____   Date _____

_____
Phonological Process

Correct Responses/Total Percentage

_____
Word/Phrase/Sentence Level

☐ ☐ ☐ ☐ ☐ ☐ ☐ ☐ ☐ = ____%

Name _____   Date _____

_____
Phonological Process

Correct Responses/Total Percentage

_____
Word/Phrase/Sentence Level

☐ ☐ ☐ ☐ ☐ ☐ ☐ ☐ ☐ = ____%

Tracking Sheet

Student Name

Date	Phonological Process	Sound	Word, Phrase, or Sentence Level	✔ or -	%	Comments

#BK-320 Webber® Photo Phonology Minimal Pair Cards Fun Sheets • ©2005 Super Duper® Publications • www.superduperinc.com • 1-800-277-8737

Auditory Bombardment

Directions: Have the student listen carefully as you read the following list of words slowly and clearly. The student does not need to repeat the words, but just listen to them. You may have the student engage in a quiet activity, like coloring, as you read.

1. soap	34. have	67. boat
2. rope	35. hive	68. hot
3. type	36. dive	69. coat
4. sheep	37. move	70. bat
5. soup	38. save	71. seed
6. pipe	39. pave	72. toad
7. cap	40. shave	73. bed
8. cup	41. race	74. mad
9. zip	42. case	75. fed
10. hop	43. face	76. kid
11. robe	44. mice	77. bead
12. cab	45. piece	78. mud
13. cub	46. moose	79. road
14. lab	47. rice	80. side
15. rib	48. ice	81. peach
16. web	49. bus	82. couch
17. cube	50. juice	83. touch
18. tub	51. bean	84. lunch
19. sub	52. moon	85. teach
20. job	53. can	86. bench
21. time	54. fin	87. catch
22. team	55. pan	88. watch
23. home	56. den	89. coach
24. comb	57. fan	90. rich
25. same	58. men	91. bike
26. gum	59. run	92. rock
27. game	60. van	93. book
28. dime	61. goat	94. knock
29. jam	62. bite	95. back
30. lamb	63. meat	96. tack
31. wave	64. boot	97. lake
32. cave	65. put	98. hook
33. give	66. feet	99. pick
		100. cake

_____	_____	_____	**Final Consonant Deletion Word Level**
Name	Date	Homework Partner	

Minimal Contrast Pairs

Directions: Have student point to picture-words as teacher/helper says each word aloud.

1. K   case

2. go   goat

3. buy   bite

4. me   meat

5. boo   boot

6. bow   boat

7. knee   neat

8. bee   bean

9. moo   moon

10. weigh   wave

_____ _____ _____

Name   Date   Homework Partner

Final Consonant Deletion Word Level

#BK-320 Webber® Photo Phonology Minimal Pair Cards Fun Sheets • ©2005 Super Duper® Publications • www.superduperinc.com • 1-800-277-8737

Minimal Contrast Pairs

Directions: Have student point to picture-words as teacher/helper says each word aloud.

1.

pea   peach

2.

cow   couch

3.

bye   bike

4.

four   fork

5.

sew   soap

6.

row   rope

7.

tie   type

8.

she   sheep

9.

Sue   soup

10.

pie   pipe

_____   _____   _____

Name   Date   Homework Partner

Final Consonant Deletion Word Level

Minimal Contrast Pairs

Directions: Have student point to picture-words as teacher/helper says each word aloud.

1.
row   robe

2.
tie   time

3.
tea   team

4.
hoe   home

5.
C   seed

6.
toe   toad

7.
Ray   race

8.
eye   ice

9.
she   sheep

10.
pie   pipe

_____   _____   _____

Name   Date   Homework Partner

Final Consonant Deletion Word Level

#BK-320 Webber® Photo Phonology Minimal Pair Cards Fun Sheets • ©2005 Super Duper® Publications • www.superduperinc.com • 1-800-277-8737

Minimal Contrast Definitions

Directions: Read each question and possible answers aloud. Ask students to circle and/or say the correct answer.

1. What is for washing?

   sew   soap

2. What do you do with a needle and thread?

   sew   soap

3. What is for tying knots?

   row   rope

4. What do you do in a boat?

   row   rope

5. What do you do at a computer?

   tie   type

6. What does the boy wear around his neck?

   tie   type

7. Which one says *"baa-baa"*?

   she   sheep

8. Which one is another name for a girl?

   she   sheep

9. Which one is a girl's name?

   Sue   soup

10. Which one do you eat with a spoon?

   Sue   soup

_____   _____   _____
Name   Date   Homework Partner

Final Consonant Deletion Word Level

Minimal Contrast Definitions

Directions: Read each question and possible answers aloud. Ask students to circle and/or say the correct answer.

1. Which one do you eat?

pie   **pipe**

2. What does water flow through?

pie   **pipe**

3. What do you wear after a bath or shower?

row   **robe**

4. What do you do in a boat?

row   **robe**

5. Which one is a boy's name?

Ray   **race**

6. What can you run in?

Ray   **race**

7. Which one holds things?

K   **case**

8. Which one is a letter?

K   **case**

9. What do you do with shoelaces?

tie   **time**

10. What does a clock tell?

tie   **time**

_____ _____ _____

Homework Partner   Date   Name

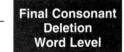

Final Consonant Deletion Word Level

#BK-320 Webber® Photo Phonology Minimal Pair Cards Fun Sheets • ©2005 Super Duper® Publications • www.superduperinc.com • 1-800-277-8737

Minimal Contrast Definitions

Directions: Read each question and possible answers aloud. Ask students to circle and/or say the correct answer.

1. Which one blinks?

eye   ice

2. Which one makes your drink cold?

eye   ice

3. What makes honey?

bee   bean

4. Which one do you eat?

bee   bean

5. Who plays a sport?

tea   team

6. What do you drink?

tea   team

7. What does a cow say?

Moo

moo   moon

8. What do you see at night?

Moo

moo   moon

9. What do you do when you see someone you know?

weigh   wave

10. Stand on a scale to see how much you...

weigh   wave

Final Consonant Deletion Word Level

_____ _____ _____
Name   Date   Homework Partner

#BK-320 Webber® Photo Phonology Minimal Pair Cards Fun Sheets • ©2005 Super Duper® Publications • www.superduperinc.com • 1-800-277-8737

Minimal Contrast Definitions

Directions: Read each question and possible answers aloud. Ask students to circle and/or say the correct answer.

1. Which is a farm animal?

go   **goat**

2. What do you do at a green light?

go   **goat**

3. What do you do with your teeth?

buy   **bite**

4. What do you do at a store?

buy   **bite**

5. What do you wear on your feet?

boo   **boot**

6. What does a ghost say?

boo   **boot**

7. What does your mom like your room to look like?

knee   **neat**

8. What is part of your body?

knee   **neat**

9. What goes on top of a present?

bow   **boat**

10. What floats on water?

bow   **boat**

_____   _____   _____

Name   Date   Homework Partner

Final Consonant Deletion Word Level

#BK-320 Webber® Photo Phonology Minimal Pair Cards Fun Sheets • ©2005 Super Duper® Publications • www.superduperinc.com • 1-800-277-8737

Minimal Contrast Definitions

Directions: Read each question and possible answers aloud. Ask students to circle and/or say the correct answer.

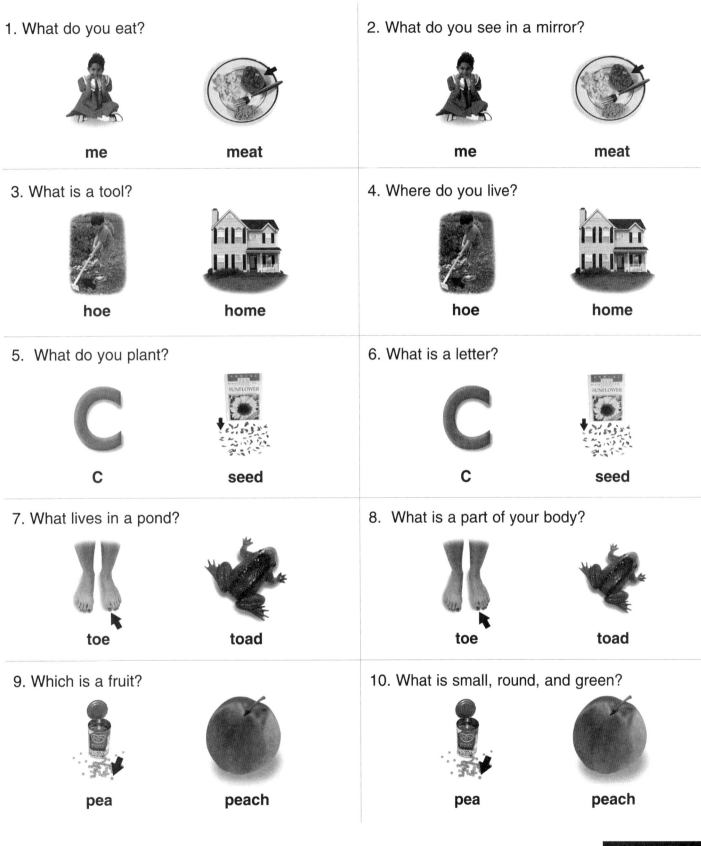

1. What do you eat?

me   meat

2. What do you see in a mirror?

me   meat

3. What is a tool?

hoe   home

4. Where do you live?

hoe   home

5. What do you plant?

C   seed

6. What is a letter?

C   seed

7. What lives in a pond?

toe   toad

8. What is a part of your body?

toe   toad

9. Which is a fruit?

pea   peach

10. What is small, round, and green?

pea   peach

_____ _____ _____

Name   Date   Homework Partner

Final Consonant Deletion Word Level

Minimal Contrast Definitions

Directions: Read each question and possible answers aloud. Ask students to circle and/or say the correct answer.

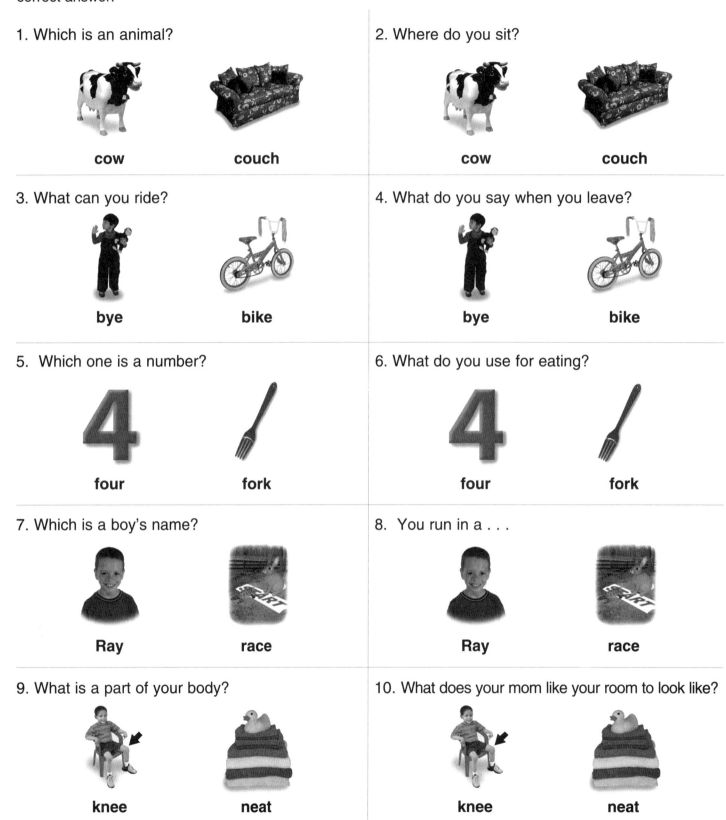

1. Which is an animal?

cow   couch

2. Where do you sit?

cow   couch

3. What can you ride?

bye   bike

4. What do you say when you leave?

bye   bike

5. Which one is a number?

four   fork

6. What do you use for eating?

four   fork

7. Which is a boy's name?

Ray   race

8. You run in a . . .

Ray   race

9. What is a part of your body?

knee   neat

10. What does your mom like your room to look like?

knee   neat

_____ _____ _____

Name   Date   Homework Partner

**Final Consonant
Deletion
Word Level**

#BK-320 Webber® Photo Phonology Minimal Pair Cards Fun Sheets • ©2005 Super Duper® Publications • www.superduperinc.com • 1-800-277-8737

Pesky Parrot

Directions: Cut out the crackers below and place them in a pile. Then, cut along the dotted line to make the parrot's mouth. Draw a card and read/say the picture-words aloud while you feed the parrot.

sew	soup
pipe	tie
soap	rope
type	Sue

| row | pie | she | C | sheep | seed |

_____ _____ _____

Name   Date   Homework Partner

Final Consonant Deletion Word Level

Memory Game

Directions: Read/say aloud each picture-word below. Cut out the pictures. Place all cards face down. Turn over cards two at a time and try to find a match. Say each card as you pick it up. Keep all matches. Most matches wins!

tie	time	tea	team
Ray	race	K	case
eye	ice	tie	time
tea	team	Ray	race
K	case	eye	ice

_____ _____ _____

Homework Partner   Date   Name

#BK-320 Webber® Photo Phonology Minimal Pair Cards Fun Sheets • ©2005 Super Duper® Publications • www.superduperinc.com • 1-800-277-8737

Hide 'n' Seek

Directions: Read/say aloud the picture-words. Cut out the pictures and penny. Place the pictures face up. Teacher/helper hides the penny under a picture. Say each picture-word as you look underneath for the penny. Find the penny and you win!

bee	bean	moo	moon
go	goat	buy	bite
me	meat	boo	boot
weigh	wave	knee	neat

_____ _____ _____

Name   Date   Homework Partner

Final Consonant Deletion Word Level

#BK-320 Webber® Photo Phonology Minimal Pair Cards Fun Sheets • ©2005 Super Duper® Publications • www.superduperinc.com • 1-800-277-8737

13

Fishy Business

Directions: Read/say aloud the words below. Then, cut out the fish. Fill the aquarium with the fish, saying the name of each picture as you place it in the aquarium.

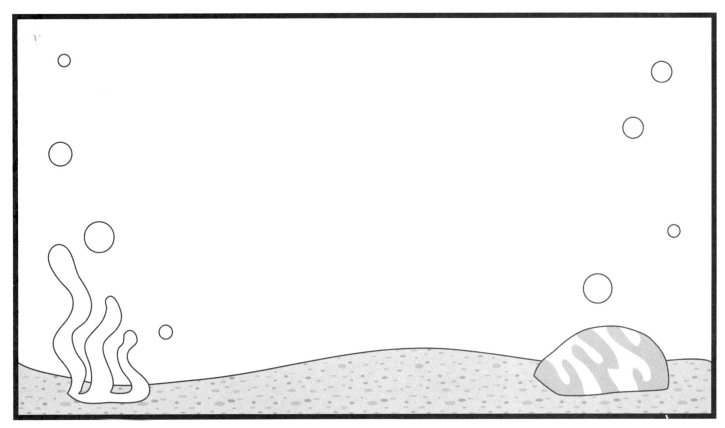

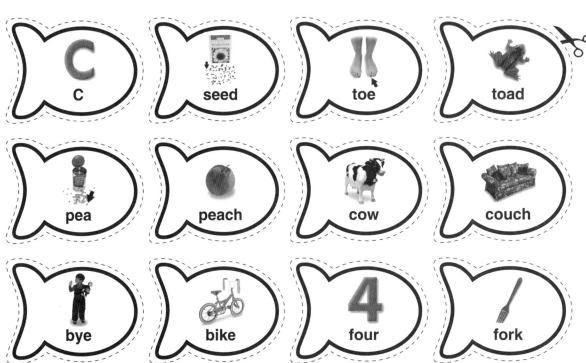

c	seed	toe	toad
pea	peach	cow	couch
bye	bike	four	fork

Name　　　　　Date　　　　　Homework Partner

#BK-320 Webber® Photo Phonology Minimal Pair Cards Fun Sheets • ©2005 Super Duper® Publications • www.superduperinc.com • 1-800-277-8737

Complete a Phrase

Directions: Complete the phrases with the correct word. Read/say the phrases aloud. Variation: Roll a die to see how many times you have to say the phrase.

1. a bowl of hot _____

2. the horns on the _____

3. a sunflower _____

4. a knot in the _____

5. a toy _____

6. a two-story _____

7. bar of _____

seed

goat

soap

boat

home

soup

rope

_____ _____ _____
Name   Date   Homework Partner

Phrase Fill-In

Directions: Write a vowel in each blank space below to spell the words correctly. Then read/say each phrase aloud.

1. r__de a b__ke

2. t__ll t__me

3. sit __n a c__uch

4. g__ n__w

5. e__t a pe__ch

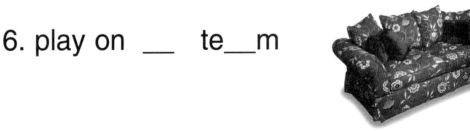

6. play on __ te__m

Answer Key: 1.i,i 2.e,i 3.o,o 4.o,o 5.a,a 6.a,a

#BK-320 Webber® Photo Phonology Minimal Pair Cards Fun Sheets • ©2005 Super Duper® Publications • www.superduperinc.com • 1-800-277-8737

_____   _____   _____
Name   Date   Homework Partner

**Final Consonant
Deletion
Phrase Level**

Shape Match

Directions: Draw a line from a shape in Column A to the one that matches it in Column B. Read/say the phrase aloud.

A

B

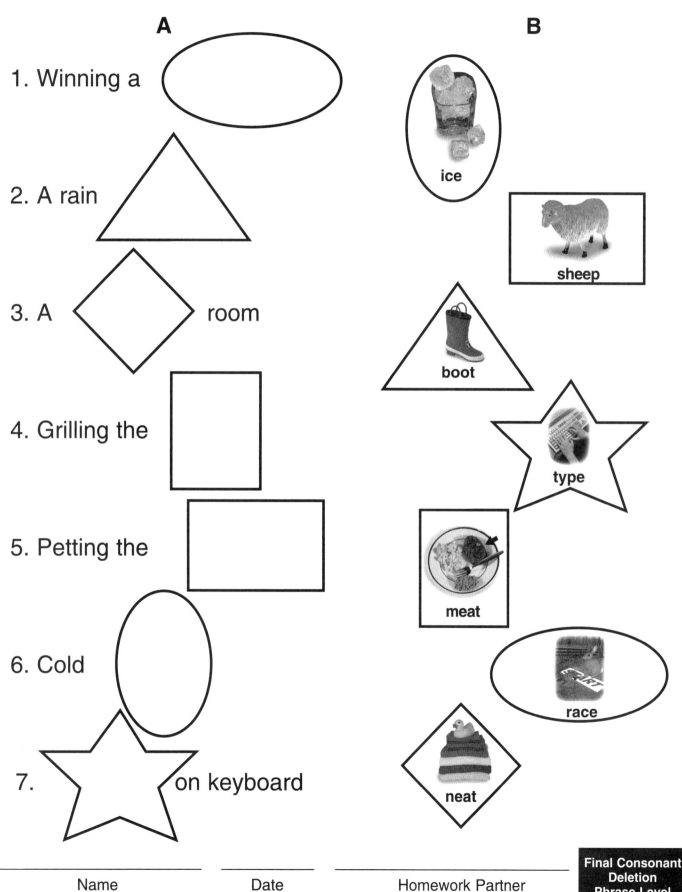

1. Winning a

2. A rain

3. A ⬦ room

4. Grilling the

5. Petting the

6. Cold

7. ★ on keyboard

ice

sheep

boot

type

meat

race

neat

Name   Date   Homework Partner

Heads or Tails

Directions: Cut out the cards below. Place them in a pile face down. Turn over a card and flip a coin. Heads means to use the picture-word in the phrase *"big_____."* Tails means to use the picture-word in the phrase *"little_____."*

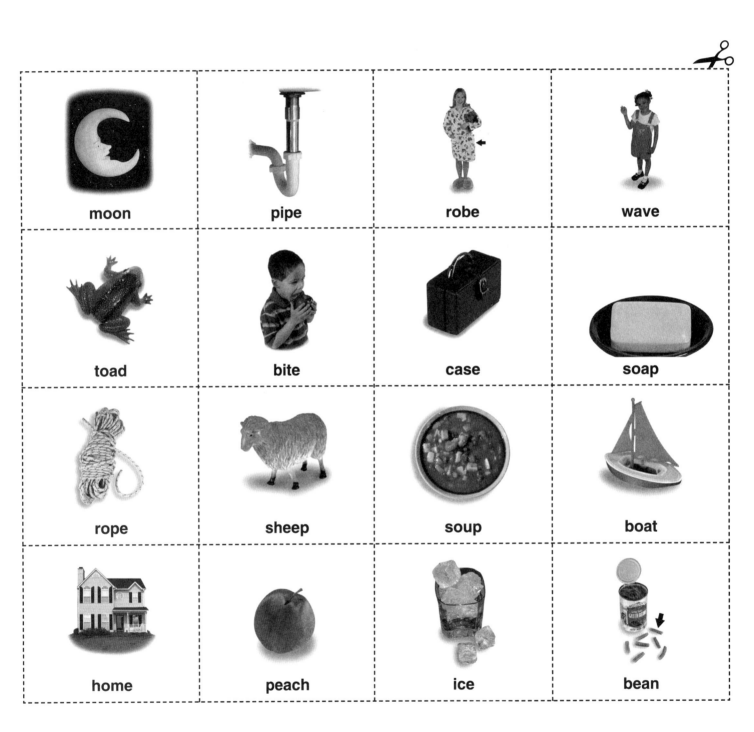

moon	pipe	robe	wave
toad	bite	case	soap
rope	sheep	soup	boat
home	peach	ice	bean

_____ _____ _____

Name   Date   Homework Partner

#BK-320 Webber® Photo Phonology Minimal Pair Cards Fun Sheets • ©2005 Super Duper® Publications • www.superduperinc.com • 1-800-277-8737

Sentence Fill-In

Directions: Draw a line from the sentence in Column A to the picture-word that completes it in Column B.

A

1. I put _____ in my drink.

2. A _____ lives on the farm.

3. I ride my _____.

4. The _____ is hot.

5. The plumber fixed the _____.

6. Wash your hands with _____.

7. The _____ sat on the lily pad.

B

toad

ice

pipe

soup

sheep

bike

soap

_____ _____ _____
Name   Date   Homework Partner

Final Consonant
Deletion
Sentence Level

Replace It

Directions: Read/say each sentence below. Using a picture-word from the Word Bank, change the underlined word in the sentence so that it makes sense. Then, read/say the corrected sentence aloud.

Word Bank

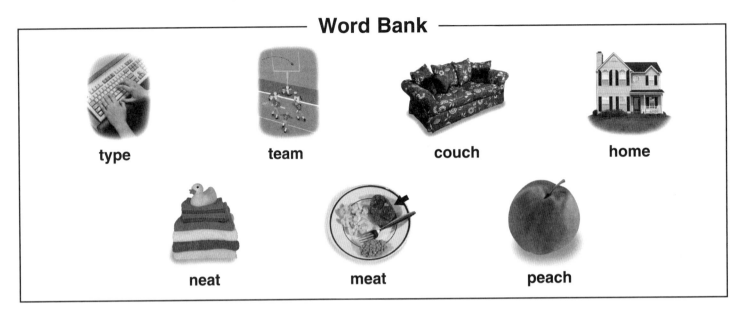

type　　　　team　　　　couch　　　　home

neat　　　　meat　　　　peach

1. A <u>nose</u> is a fruit.

2. I played on the basketball <u>store</u>.

3. Keep your room <u>tall</u>.

4. <u>Sleep</u> on the computer.

5. I want to go <u>chair</u>.

6. He sat on the <u>shelf</u>.

7. Use a knife to cut the <u>water</u>.

Answer Key: 1. peach　2. team　3. neat　4. type　5. home　6. couch　7. meat

Toy Store

Directions: Read/say aloud the picture-words on the shelves. Cut out the dollar bills below. Give a dollar bill to your teacher/homework partner as you pick out something to buy. Say, *"I want to buy (a) _____."*

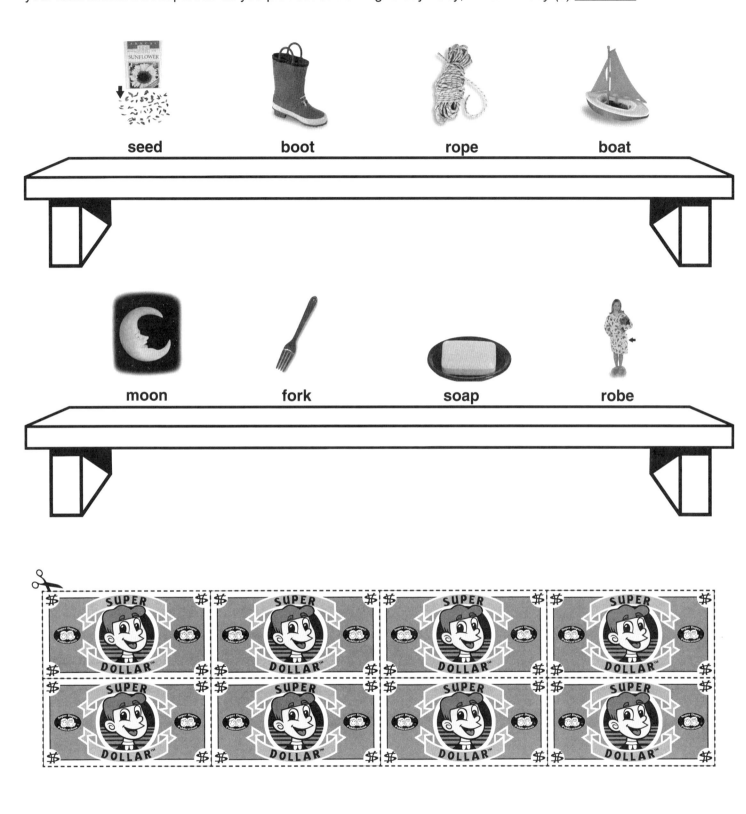

seed   boot   rope   boat

moon   fork   soap   robe

_____   _____   _____

Name   Date   Homework Partner

#BK-320 Webber® Photo Phonology Minimal Pair Cards Fun Sheets • ©2005 Super Duper® Publications • www.superduperinc.com • 1-800-277-8737

Final Consonant Deletion Sentence Level

Story Loop

Directions: Read/say aloud each picture-word. Make up a story using all of the pictures in the circle. You can start anywhere in the circle and go in either direction, but you must always end where you started to complete the loop. Say your story aloud.

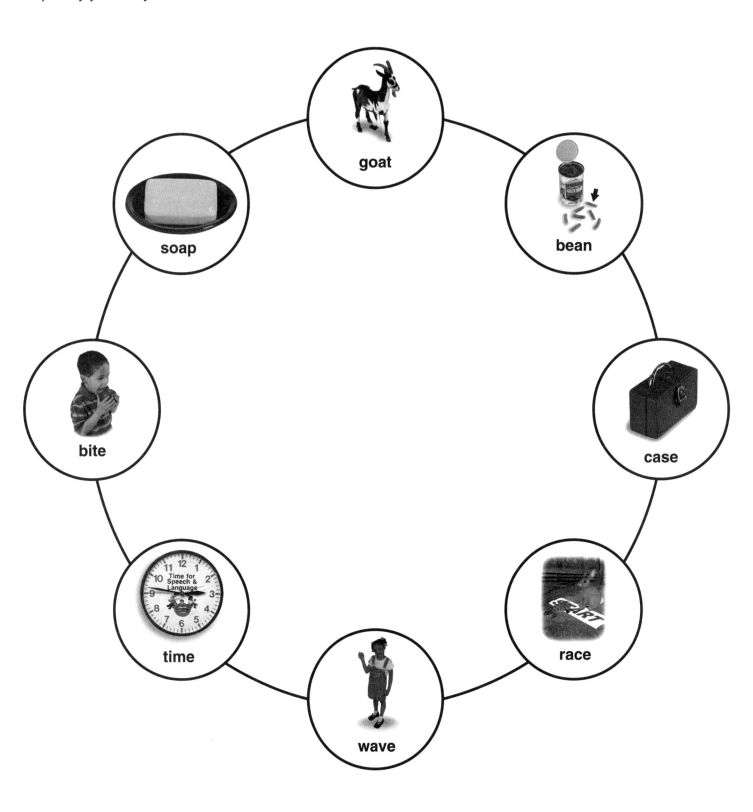

_____ _____ _____

Name   Date   Homework Partner

#BK-320 Webber® Photo Phonology Minimal Pair Cards Fun Sheets • ©2005 Super Duper® Publications • www.superduperinc.com • 1-800-277-8737

Auditory Bombardment

Directions: Have the student listen carefully as you read the following list of words slowly and clearly. The student does not need to repeat the words, but just listen to them. You may have the student engage in a quiet activity, like coloring, as you read.

1. key	34. cow	67. gate
2. cape	35. cut	68. go
3. cub	36. cup	69. guy
4. call	37. curl	70. game
5. cake	38. curve	71. girl
6. cap	39. kid	72. goose
7. can	40. king	73. gold
8. cab	41. kiss	74. gum
9. calf	42. kite	75. beg
10. camp	43. back	76. bug
11. cane	44. sick	77. mug
12. car	45. sack	78. egg
13. card	46. bike	79. fig
14. cart	47. pack	80. hog
15. case	48. book	81. jug
16. cash	49. buck	82. pig
17. cast	50. deck	83. rug
18. cat	51. dock	84. tag
19. cave	52. duck	85. wig
20. coach	53. joke	86. shine
21. coal	54. lake	87. ship
22. coat	55. lick	88. show
23. cob	56. like	89. shower
24. coin	57. luck	90. shoe
25. colt	58. neck	91. shave
26. comb	59. quack	92. shell
27. cone	60. rake	93. shade
28. cool	61. rock	94. shake
29. core	62. sock	95. shed
30. corn	63. truck	96. shelf
31. cot	64. walk	97. shirt
32. couch	65. gear	98. shop
33. cough	66. gown	99. shout
		100. shy

_____ _____ _____

Name Date Homework Partner

Fronting Word Level

#BK-320 Webber® Photo Phonology Minimal Pair Cards Fun Sheets • ©2005 Super Duper® Publications • www.superduperinc.com • 1-800-277-8737

23

Minimal Contrast Pairs

Directions: Have student point to picture-words as teacher/helper says each word aloud.

1.

tea   key

2.

tape   cape

3.

tub   cub

4.

tall   call

5.

take   cake

6.

tap   cap

7.

tan   can

8.

bat   back

9.

sit   sick

10.

sat   sack

_____   _____   _____

Name   Date   Homework Partner

Fronting Word Level

#BK-320 Webber® Photo Phonology Minimal Pair Cards Fun Sheets • ©2005 Super Duper® Publications • www.superduperinc.com • 1-800-277-8737

Minimal Contrast Pairs

Directions: Have student point to picture-words as teacher/helper says each word aloud.

1. bite | bike

2. deer | gear

3. down | gown

4. date | gate

5. dough | go

6. die | guy

7. bed | beg

8. bud | bug

9. mud | mug

10. Ed | egg

Name _____ Date _____ Homework Partner _____

Minimal Contrast Pairs

Directions: Have student point to picture-words as teacher/helper says each word aloud.

1.

sign   shine

2.

sip   ship

3.

sew   show

4.

sour   shower

5.

Sue   shoe

6.

save   shave

7.

sell   shell

8.

pat   pack

9.

bite   bike

10.

sit   sick

_____   _____   _____

Name   Date   Homework Partner

Fronting Word Level

#BK-320 Webber® Photo Phonology Minimal Pair Cards Fun Sheets • ©2005 Super Duper® Publications • www.superduperinc.com • 1-800-277-8737

Minimal Contrast Definitions

Directions: Read each question and possible answers aloud. Ask students to circle and/or say the correct answer.

1. Which one opens a door?

tea　　　　　**key**

2. What do you drink?

tea　　　　　**key**

3. What is sticky and holds things together?

tape　　　　　**cape**

4. What does Superman wear?

tape　　　　　**cape**

5. Which one is for taking a bath?

tub　　　　　**cub**

6. What is a baby tiger called?

tub　　　　　**cub**

7. Use a phone to make a ...

tall　　　　　**call**

8. What is the opposite of "short"?

tall　　　　　**call**

9. What do you make out of flour and eggs?

take　　　　　**cake**

10. With a camera, you _____ a picture.

take　　　　　**cake**

_____ _____ _____

Name　　　　　　　Date　　　　　Homework Partner

Fronting Word Level

Minimal Contrast Definitions

Directions: Read each question and possible answers aloud. Ask students to circle and/or say the correct answer.

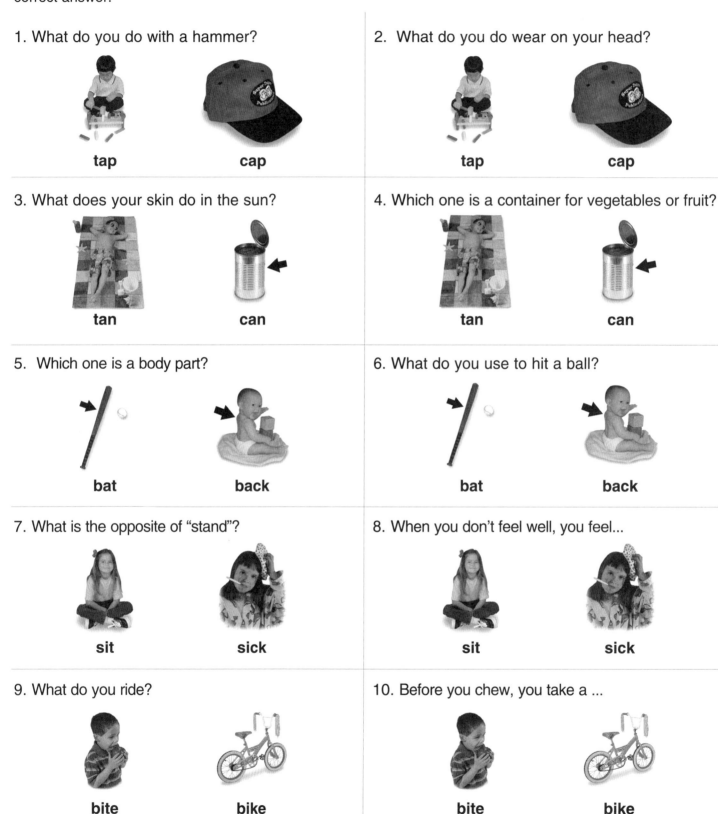

1. What do you do with a hammer?

   tap   **cap**

2. What do you do wear on your head?

   tap   **cap**

3. What does your skin do in the sun?

   tan   **can**

4. Which one is a container for vegetables or fruit?

   tan   **can**

5. Which one is a body part?

   bat   **back**

6. What do you use to hit a ball?

   bat   **back**

7. What is the opposite of "stand"?

   sit   **sick**

8. When you don't feel well, you feel...

   sit   **sick**

9. What do you ride?

   bite   **bike**

10. Before you chew, you take a ...

    bite   **bike**

_____   _____   _____

Name   Date   Homework Partner

Fronting Word Level

#BK-320 Webber® Photo Phonology Minimal Pair Cards Fun Sheets • ©2005 Super Duper® Publications • www.superduperinc.com • 1-800-277-8737

Minimal Contrast Definitions

Directions: Read each question and possible answers aloud. Ask students to circle and/or say the correct answer.

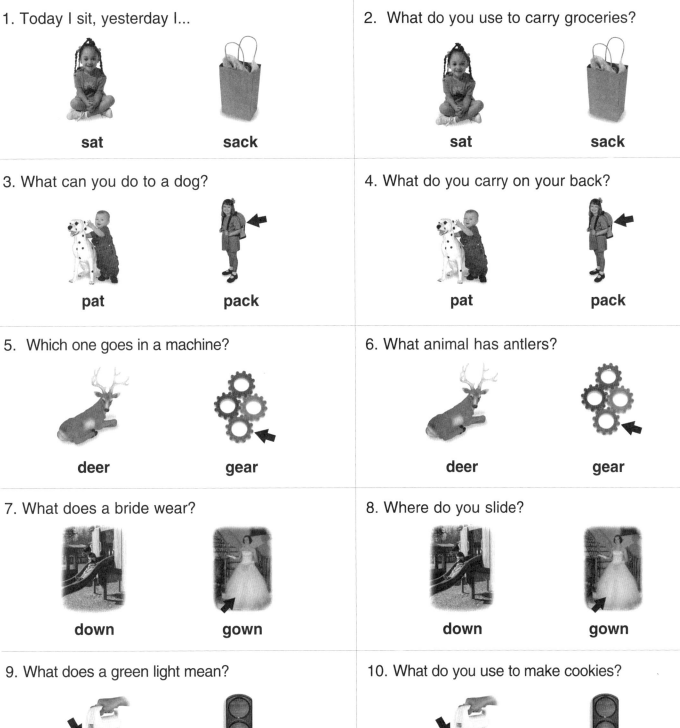

1. Today I sit, yesterday I...

sat   **sack**

2. What do you use to carry groceries?

sat   **sack**

3. What can you do to a dog?

pat   **pack**

4. What do you carry on your back?

pat   **pack**

5. Which one goes in a machine?

deer   **gear**

6. What animal has antlers?

deer   **gear**

7. What does a bride wear?

down   **gown**

8. Where do you slide?

down   **gown**

9. What does a green light mean?

dough   **go**

10. What do you use to make cookies?

dough   **go**

_____ _____ _____

Name   Date   Homework Partner

Fronting Word Level

Minimal Contrast Definitions

Directions: Read each question and possible answers aloud. Ask students to circle and/or say the correct answer.

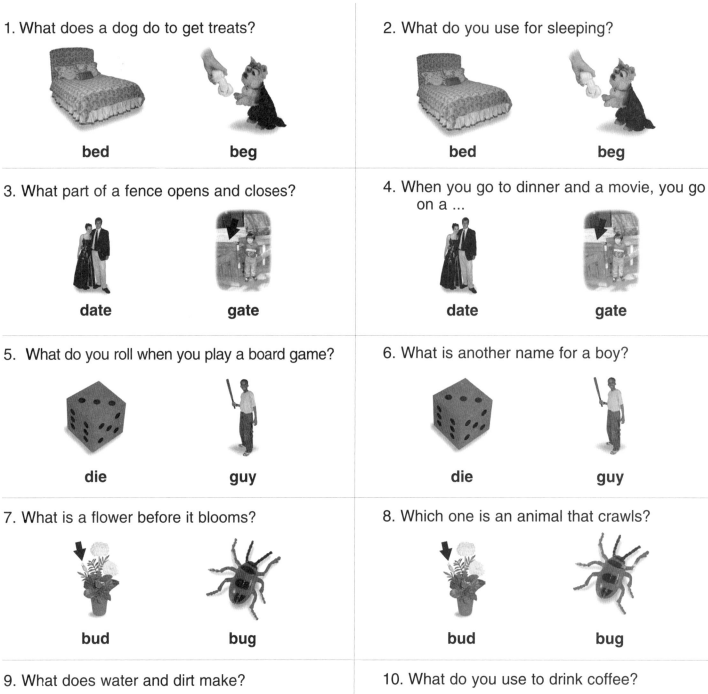

1. What does a dog do to get treats?

bed   **beg**

2. What do you use for sleeping?

bed   **beg**

3. What part of a fence opens and closes?

date   **gate**

4. When you go to dinner and a movie, you go on a ...

date   **gate**

5. What do you roll when you play a board game?

die   **guy**

6. What is another name for a boy?

die   **guy**

7. What is a flower before it blooms?

bud   **bug**

8. Which one is an animal that crawls?

bud   **bug**

9. What does water and dirt make?

mud   **mug**

10. What do you use to drink coffee?

mud   **mug**

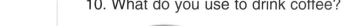

Name   Date   Homework Partner

Fronting Word Level

#BK-320 Webber® Photo Phonology Minimal Pair Cards Fun Sheets • ©2005 Super Duper® Publications • www.superduperinc.com • 1-800-277-8737

Minimal Contrast Definitions

Directions: Read each question and possible answers aloud. Ask students to circle and/or say the correct answer.

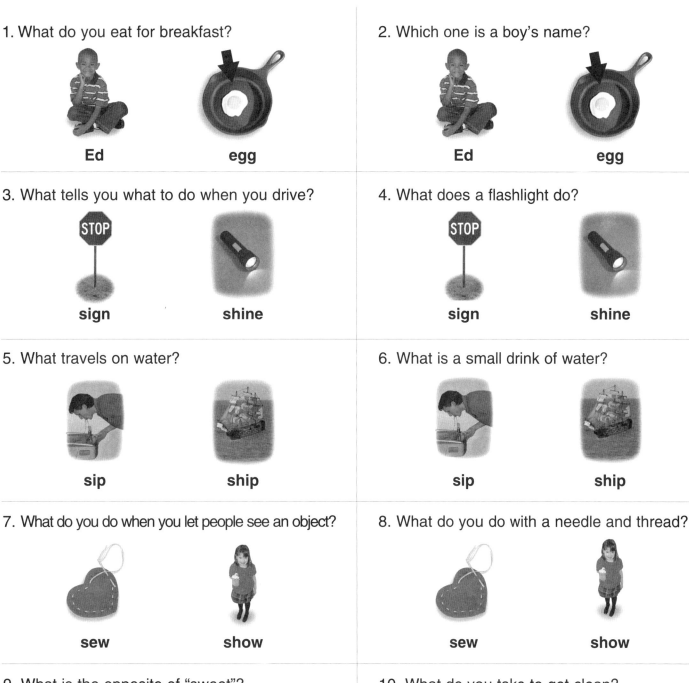

1. What do you eat for breakfast?

   Ed   **egg**

2. Which one is a boy's name?

   Ed   **egg**

3. What tells you what to do when you drive?

   sign   **shine**

4. What does a flashlight do?

   sign   **shine**

5. What travels on water?

   sip   **ship**

6. What is a small drink of water?

   sip   **ship**

7. What do you do when you let people see an object?

   sew   **show**

8. What do you do with a needle and thread?

   sew   **show**

9. What is the opposite of "sweet"?

   sour   **shower**

10. What do you take to get clean?

   sour   **shower**

_____ _____ _____

Name   Date   Homework Partner

Fronting Word Level

Minimal Contrast Definitions

Directions: Read each question and possible answers aloud. Ask students to circle and/or say the correct answer.

1. What do you wear on your foot?

shoe　　　　　　**Sue**

2. Which one is a girl's name?

shoe　　　　　　**Sue**

3. What does a man do with shaving cream and a razor?

save　　　　　　**shave**

4. What do you use a piggy bank to do?

save　　　　　　**shave**

5. What do you do at a lemonade stand?

sell　　　　　　**shell**

6. What do you find at the beach?

sell　　　　　　**shell**

7. Before you chew, you take a ...

bite　　　　　　**bike**

8. What do you ride?

bite　　　　　　**bike**

9. What is the opposite of "short"?

tall　　　　　　**call**

10. Use a phone to make a ...

tall　　　　　　**call**

Fronting
Word Level

_____ _____ _____

Name　　　　　　Date　　　　　　Homework Partner

Hungry Hippo

Directions: Cut out the picture-word cards below and place them in a pile. Then, cut along the dotted line to make the hippo's mouth. Draw a card and read/say the picture-words aloud while you feed the hippo.

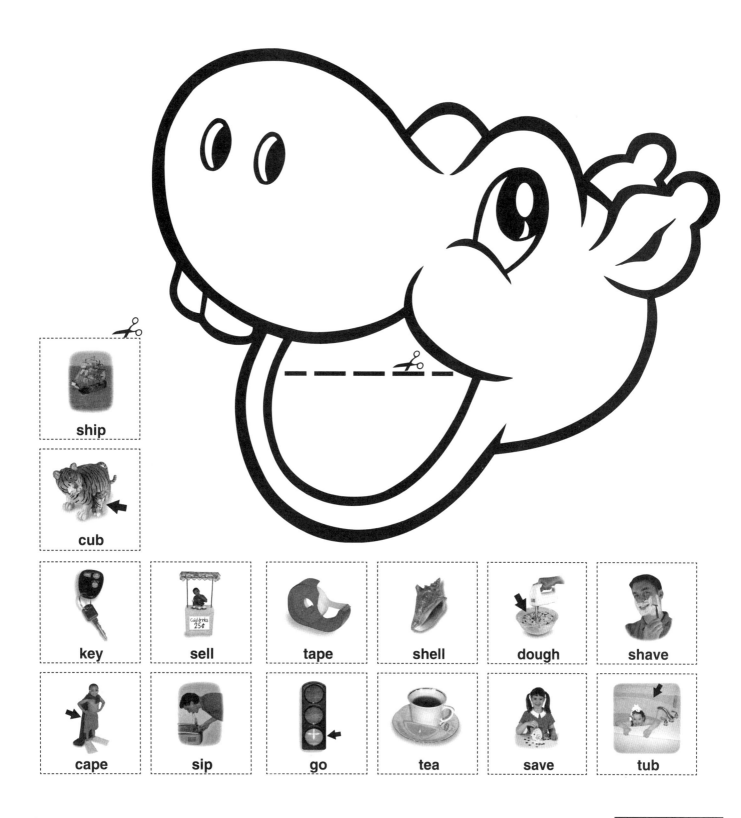

ship

cub

key	sell	tape	shell	dough	shave
cape	sip	go	tea	save	tub

Match Up

Directions: Read/say aloud each picture-word below. Cut out the pictures. Place all cards face down. Turn over two cards and try to make a match. Say each card as you pick it up. Keep all matches. Most matches wins!

bat	back	sit	sick
sour	shower	bite	bike
pat	pack	bat	back
sit	sick	sour	shower
bite	bike	pat	pack

_____ _____ _____

Name Date Homework Partner

#BK-320 Webber® Photo Phonology Minimal Pair Cards Fun Sheets • ©2005 Super Duper® Publications • www.superduperinc.com • 1-800-277-8737

Hide 'n' Seek

Directions: Read/say aloud the picture-words. Cut out the pictures and penny. Place the pictures face up. Teacher/helper hides the penny under a picture. Say each picture-word as you look underneath for the penny. Find the penny and you win!

date	gate	tan	can
sell	shell	bed	beg
bud	bug	tall	call
Ed	egg	sat	sack

#BK-320 Webber® Photo Phonology Minimal Pair Cards Fun Sheets • ©2005 Super Duper® Publications • www.superduperinc.com • 1-800-277-8737

Cookie Craze

Directions: Cut out the cookies and place them face down in a pile. As you turn over each cookie, read/say aloud each picture-word and glue, tape, or place the cookie on the jar.

sign

shine

take

cake

deer

gear

sat

sack

Sue

shoe

_____ _____ _____ _____
Name   Date   Homework Partner

Fronting
Word Level

X and O

Directions: Cut out each X and O below. Have each player/partner choose X or O. The first player reads/ says a picture-phrase aloud and places an X or O on the square. Play continues in turn. The first person to get three in a row wins.

finding a shell	a baseball cap	ready, set, go
the tin can	a telephone call	a magic cape
a warm shower	feeling sick	a crawling bug

_____ _____ _____

Name   Date   Homework Partner

Phrase Fill-In

Directions: Write a vowel in each blank space below to spell the words correctly. Then read/say each phrase aloud.

1. w__ar a g__wn

2. sh__w and t__ll

3. a p__ck of b__oks

4. cl__se the g__te

5. b__g for a b__ne

6. a n__w sh__e

Answer Key: 1. e, o 2. o, e 3. a, o 4. o, a 5. e, o 6. e, o

Fronting
Phrase Level

#BK-320 Webber® Photo Phonology Minimal Pair Cards Fun Sheets • ©2005 Super Duper® Publications • www.superduperinc.com • 1-800-277-8737

Puzzle Match

Directions: Draw a line from a puzzle piece in Column A to the one that matches it in Column B. Read/say the phrase aloud.

A

B

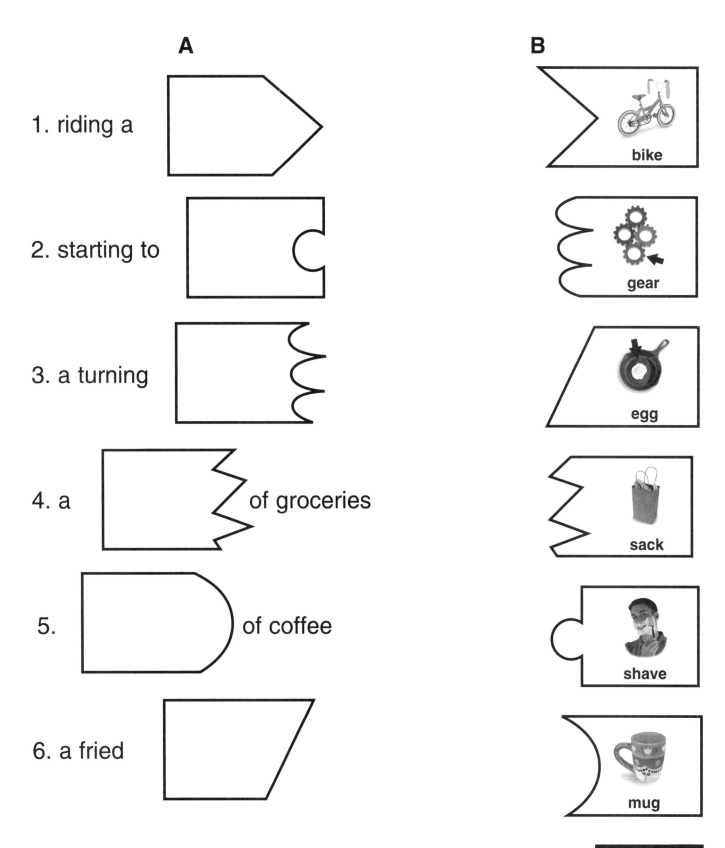

1. riding a

2. starting to

3. a turning

4. a   of groceries

5.   of coffee

6. a fried

bike

gear

egg

sack

shave

mug

_____ _____ _____

Name   Date   Homework Partner

Fronting
Phrase Level

Heads or Tails

Directions: Cut out the cards below. Place them in a pile face down. Turn over a card and flip a coin. Heads means to use the picture-word in the phrase *"big_____."* Tails means to use the picture-word in the phrase *"little_____."*

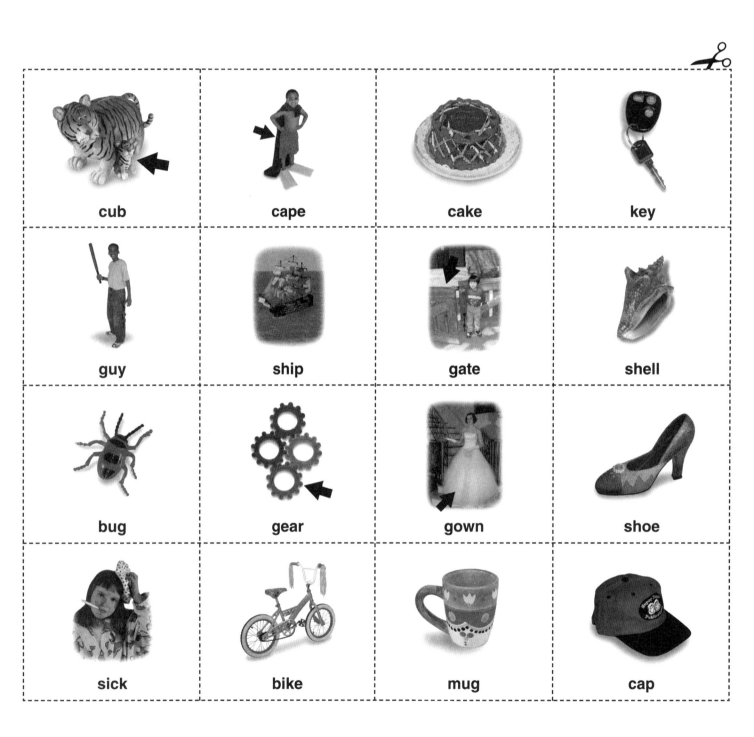

cub	cape	cake	key
guy	ship	gate	shell
bug	gear	gown	shoe
sick	bike	mug	cap

Sentence Fill-In

Directions: Draw a line from the sentence in Column A to the picture-word that completes it in Column B.

A

1. The flashlight will _____ in the dark.

2. The long _____ opens the door.

3. The baby sleeps on his _____.

4. Change the _____ to go faster.

5. The dog will _____ for bones.

6. Watch the _____ on the sea.

7. A superhero wears a _____.

B

gear

back

ship

shine

cape

key

beg

_____ _____ _____
Name   Date   Homework Partner

Fronting Sentence Level

Replace It

Directions: Read/say each sentence below. Using a picture-word from the Word Bank, change the underlined word in the sentence so that it makes sense. Then, read/say the corrected sentence aloud.

Word Bank

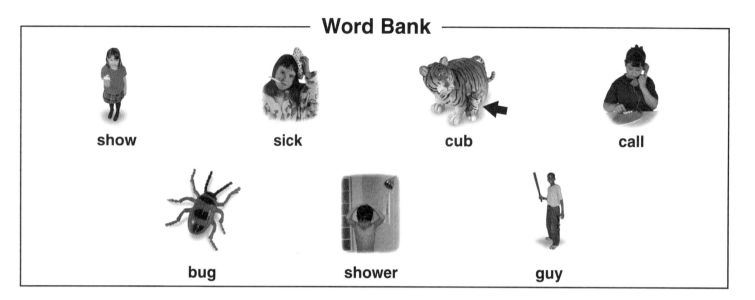

show   sick   cub   call

bug   shower   guy

1. A <u>duckling</u> is a baby tiger.

2. When you are <u>happy</u>, you may have a fever.

3. <u>Throw</u> us your report card.

4. A <u>cat</u> is an insect.

5. Take a <u>jog</u> to get clean.

6. This <u>can</u> plays baseball.

7. You have a phone <u>chair</u>.

Answer Key: 1. cub 2. sick 3. show 4. bug 5. shower 6. guy 7. call

#BK-320 Webber® Photo Phonology Minimal Pair Cards Fun Sheets • ©2005 Super Duper® Publications • www.superduperinc.com • 1-800-277-8737

Name   Date   Homework Partner

Fronting
Sentence Level

Toy Store

Directions: Read/say aloud the picture-words on the shelves. Cut out the dollar bills below. Give a dollar bill to your teacher/homework partner as you pick out something to buy. Say, *"I want to buy a _____."*

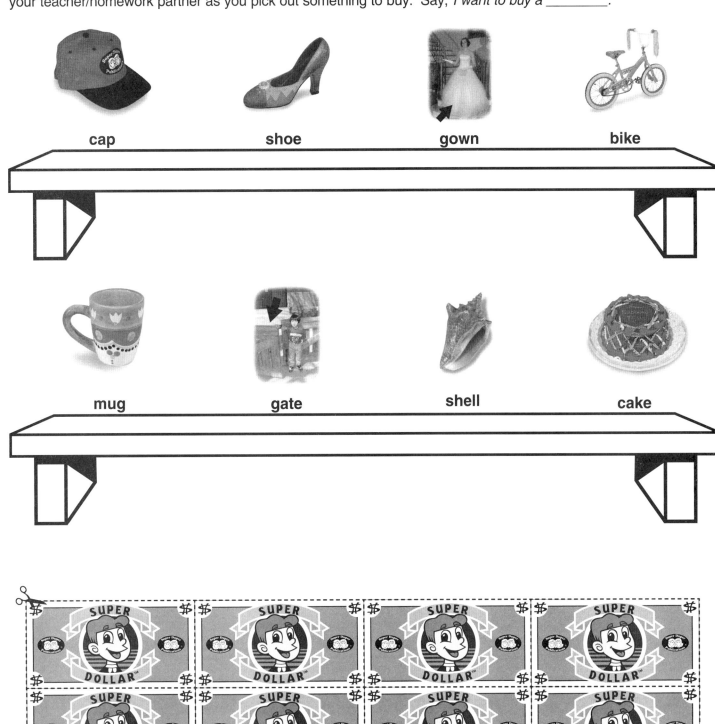

cap	shoe	gown	bike

mug	gate	shell	cake

Story Loop

Directions: Read/say aloud each picture-word. Make up a story using all of the pictures in the circle. You can start anywhere in the circle and go in either direction, but you must always end where you started to complete the loop. Say your story aloud.

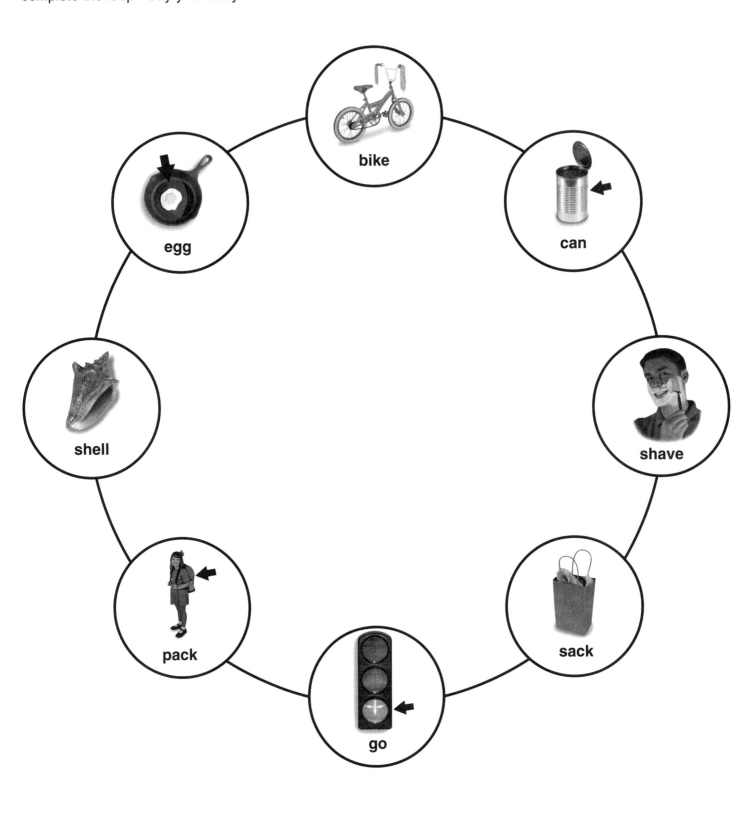

Name   Date   Homework Partner

Fronting Sentence Level

44   #BK-320 Webber® Photo Phonology Minimal Pair Cards Fun Sheets • ©2005 Super Duper® Publications • www.superduperinc.com • 1-800-277-8737

Auditory Bombardment

Directions: Have the student listen carefully as you read the following list of words slowly and clearly. The student does not need to repeat the words, but just listen to them. You may have the student engage in a quiet activity, like coloring, as you read.

1. sail	34. cross	67. wash
2. cent	35. class	68. fish
3. sack	36. house	69. wish
4. sew	37. grass	70. cash
5. sip	38. loose	71. chair
6. sock	39. mice	72. chin
7. sit	40. pass	73. chain
8. sun	41. moss	74. chase
9. surf	42. rice	75. chip
10. seed	43. mouse	76. lunch
11. sell	44. toss	77. teach
12. set	45. yes	78. peach
13. salt	46. voice	79. beach
14. soup	47. place	80. coach
15. seal	48. rose	81. thigh
16. soap	49. bees	82. thin
17. sad	50. eyes	83. thick
18. safe	51. breeze	84. math
19. sand	52. maze	85. path
20. sing	53. jazz	86. moth
21. sea	54. shake	87. four
22. side	55. shoe	88. full
23. soak	56. shop	89. fork
24. sour	57. shape	90. fan
25. sound	58. sheep	91. fun
26. south	59. shine	92. food
27. kiss	60. ship	93. leaf
28. miss	61. show	94. cuff
29. nice	62. shower	95. laugh
30. ace	63. shave	96. rough
31. boss	64. shell	97. beef
32. bus	65. shade	98. calf
33. goose	66. shed	99. cliff
		100. stuff

Stopping Word Level

_____   _____   _____

Name   Date   Homework Partner

#BK-320 Webber® Photo Phonology Minimal Pair Cards Fun Sheets • ©2005 Super Duper® Publications • www.superduperinc.com • 1-800-277-8737

Minimal Contrast Pairs

Directions: Have student point to picture-words as teacher/helper says each word aloud.

1. tail   sail

2. tent   cent

3. tack   sack

4. toe   sew

5. tip   sip

6. kit   kiss

7. mitt   miss

8. knight   nice

9. road   rose

10. bead   bees

_____ _____ _____

Name   Date   Homework Partner

Stopping Word Level

#BK-320 Webber® Photo Phonology Minimal Pair Cards Fun Sheets • ©2005 Super Duper® Publications • www.superduperinc.com • 1-800-277-8737

Minimal Contrast Pairs

Directions: Have student point to picture-words as teacher/helper says each word aloud.

1. take — shake

2. two — shoe

3. top — shop

4. tape — shape

5. cat — cash

6. tear — chair

7. coat — coach

8. beet — beach

9. tie — thigh

10. Matt — math

_____ _____ _____

Name Date Homework Partner

Stopping
Word Level

Minimal Contrast Pairs

Directions: Have student point to picture-words as teacher/helper says each word aloud.

1. pull | full

2. pour | four

3. pork | fork

4. pan | fan

5. pig | fig

6. leap | leaf

7. cup | cuff

8. lap | laugh

9. top | shop

10. mitt | miss

_____ _____ _____

Name   Date   Homework Partner

Stopping
Word Level

#BK-320 Webber® Photo Phonology Minimal Pair Cards Fun Sheets • ©2005 Super Duper® Publications • www.superduperinc.com • 1-800-277-8737

Minimal Contrast Definitions

Directions: Read each question and possible answers aloud. Ask students to circle and/or say the correct answer.

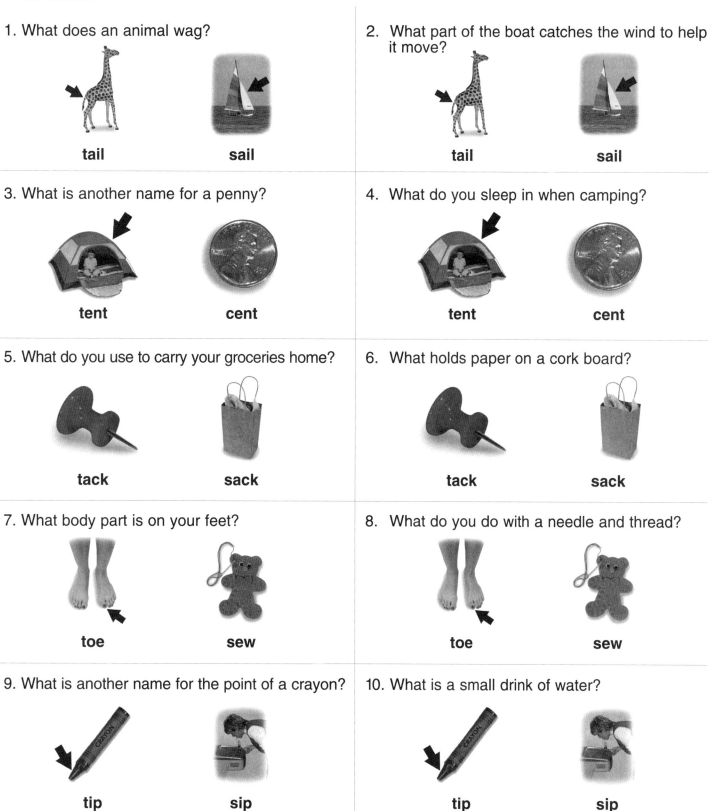

1. What does an animal wag?

tail   sail

2. What part of the boat catches the wind to help it move?

tail   sail

3. What is another name for a penny?

tent   cent

4. What do you sleep in when camping?

tent   cent

5. What do you use to carry your groceries home?

tack   sack

6. What holds paper on a cork board?

tack   sack

7. What body part is on your feet?

toe   sew

8. What do you do with a needle and thread?

toe   sew

9. What is another name for the point of a crayon?

tip   sip

10. What is a small drink of water?

tip   sip

_____ _____ _____
Name   Date   Homework Partner

Stopping Word Level

Minimal Contrast Definitions

Directions: Read each question and possible answers aloud. Ask students to circle and/or say the correct answer.

1. What happens when you do not make it in the basket?

    mitt   **miss**

2. What glove does a catcher use?

    mitt   **miss**

3. What does a doctor use to carry his equipment?

    kit   **kiss**

4. What does a princess do to a frog?

    kit   **kiss**

5. When you give someone a present, you are being...

    nice   **knight**

6. Which one wears armor?

    nice   **knight**

7. Where do cars and trucks ride?

    road   **rose**

8. Which one is a flower?

    road   **rose**

9. What insects make honey?

    bead   **bees**

10. What can be used to make a necklace?

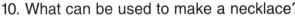

    bead   **bees**

_____ _____ _____
Name   Date   Homework Partner

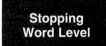

Stopping Word Level

#BK-320 Webber® Photo Phonology Minimal Pair Cards Fun Sheets • ©2005 Super Duper® Publications • www.superduperinc.com • 1-800-277-8737

Minimal Contrast Definitions

Directions: Read each question and possible answers aloud. Ask students to circle and/or say the correct answer.

1. What is an ice cream drink?

    take   shake

2. With a camera, you _____ a picture.

    take   shake

3. Which one is a number?

    two   shoe

4. What do you wear on your feet?

    two   shoe

5. What do you do at the mall?

    top   shop

6. Which one is a toy?

    top   shop

7. What is sticky and holds things together?

    tape   shape

8. What is a square, a circle, or a triangle?

    tape   shape

9. What is another name for money?

    cat   cash

10. What animal says "meow"?

    cat   cash

_____ _____ _____

Name   Date   Homework Partner

Stopping Word Level

Minimal Contrast Definitions

Directions: Read each question and possible answers aloud. Ask students to circle and/or say the correct answer.

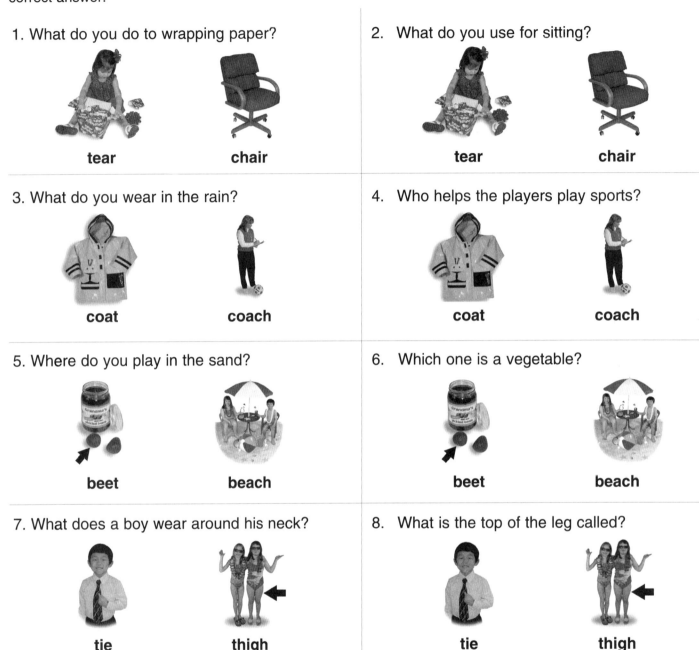

1. What do you do to wrapping paper?

   tear   **chair**

2. What do you use for sitting?

   tear   **chair**

3. What do you wear in the rain?

   coat   **coach**

4. Who helps the players play sports?

   coat   **coach**

5. Where do you play in the sand?

   beet   **beach**

6. Which one is a vegetable?

   beet   **beach**

7. What does a boy wear around his neck?

   tie   **thigh**

8. What is the top of the leg called?

   tie   **thigh**

9. What subject includes adding numbers?

   Matt   **math**

10. Which one is a boy's name?

    Matt   **math**

_____ _____ _____

Name   Date   Homework Partner

Stopping Word Level

#BK-320 Webber® Photo Phonology Minimal Pair Cards Fun Sheets • ©2005 Super Duper® Publications • www.superduperinc.com • 1-800-277-8737

Minimal Contrast Definitions

Directions: Read each question and possible answers aloud. Ask students to circle and/or say the correct answer.

1. What is the opposite of "empty"?

pull   **full**

2. What do you do with a wagon?

pull   **full**

3. Which one is a number?

pour   **four**

4. What do you do with a pitcher of juice?

pour   **four**

5. Which one is an eating utensil?

pork   **fork**

6. Which one is meat?

pork   **fork**

7. What do you use to cook?

pan   **fan**

8. What blows the air?

pan   **fan**

9. Which one is a fruit?

pig   **fig**

10. What animal says "oink oink"?

pig   **fig**

_____ _____ _____

Name   Date   Homework Partner

Stopping Word Level

Minimal Contrast Definitions

Directions: Read each question and possible answers aloud. Ask students to circle and/or say the correct answer.

1. What is another name for "jump"?

leap   **leaf**

2. What grows on a tree?

leap   **leaf**

3. What do you use for drinking?

cup   **cuff**

4. What is at the end of your sleeve?

cup   **cuff**

5. A baby sits on his dad's ...

lap   **laugh**

6. What do you do when something is funny?

lap   **laugh**

7. What is a small drink of water?

tip   **sip**

8. What is another name for the point of your crayon?

tip   **sip**

9. What do you do with a pitcher of juice?

pour   **four**

10. Which one is a number?

pour   **four**

_____ _____ _____

Name   Date   Homework Partner

#BK-320 Webber® Photo Phonology Minimal Pair Cards Fun Sheets • ©2005 Super Duper® Publications • www.superduperinc.com • 1-800-277-8737

Silly Seal

Directions: Read/say aloud the picture-words below. Then, cut out the fish. Cut dotted line at seal's mouth. Say each picture-word on the fish as you feed the seal.

tail

sail

kit

kiss

road

rose

take

shake

cat

cash

pull

full

leap

leaf

_____   _____   _____
Name   Date   Homework Partner

#BK-320 Webber® Photo Phonology Minimal Pair Cards Fun Sheets • ©2005 Super Duper® Publications • www.superduperinc.com • 1-800-277-8737

Memory Game

Directions: Read/say aloud each picture-word below. Cut out the pictures. Place all cards face down. Turn over cards two at a time and try to find a match. Say each card as you pick it up. Keep all matches. Most matches wins!

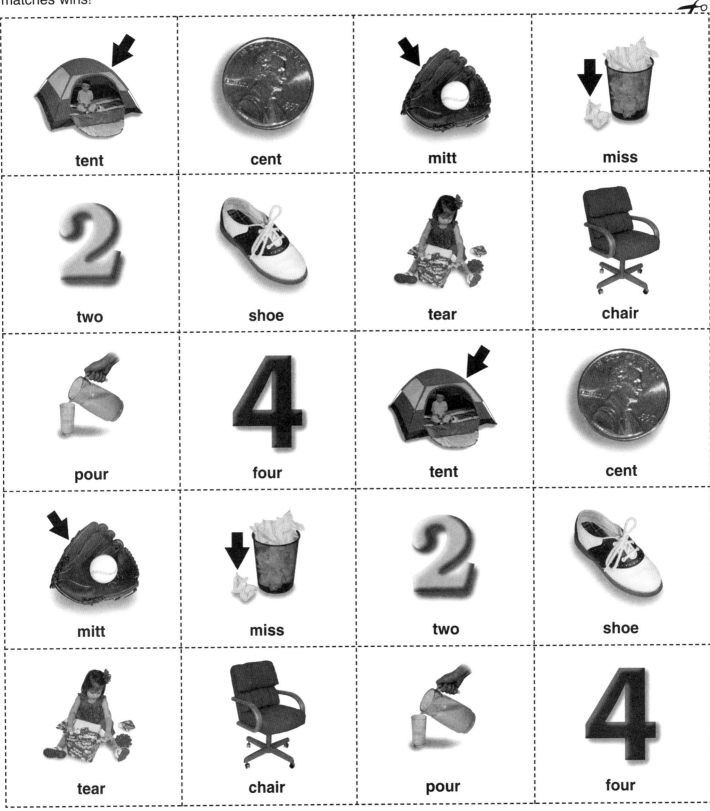

tent | cent | mitt | miss

two | shoe | tear | chair

pour | four | tent | cent

mitt | miss | two | shoe

tear | chair | pour | four

Name

Date

Homework Partner

#BK-320 Webber® Photo Phonology Minimal Pair Cards Fun Sheets • ©2005 Super Duper® Publications • www.superduperinc.com • 1-800-277-8737

Hide 'n' Seek

Directions: Read/say aloud the picture-words. Cut out the pictures and penny. Place the pictures face up. Teacher/helper hides the penny under a picture. Say each picture-word as you look underneath for the penny. Find the penny and you win!

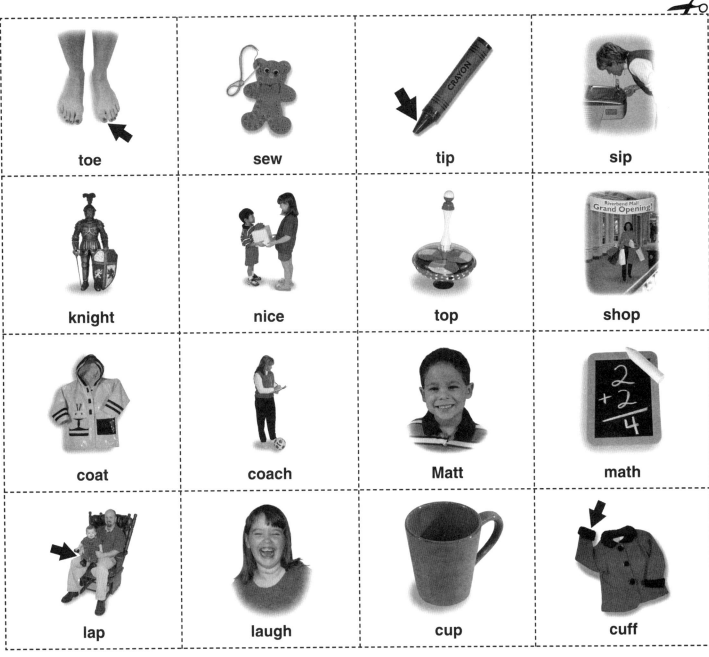

toe	sew	tip	sip
knight	nice	top	shop
coat	coach	Matt	math
lap	laugh	cup	cuff

Fig Fun

Directions: Cut out the figs and place them face down in a pile. As you choose a fig, read/say aloud each picture-word on it and glue, tape, or place the fig on the jar.

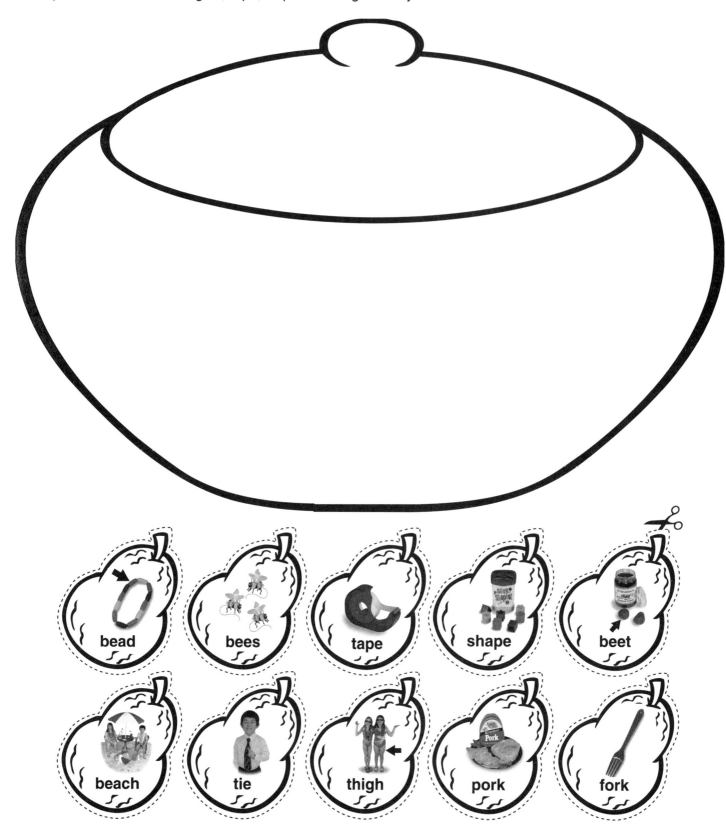

bead

bees

tape

shape

beet

beach

tie

thigh

pork

fork

Name

Date

Homework Partner

#BK-320 Webber® Photo Phonology Minimal Pair Cards Fun Sheets • ©2005 Super Duper® Publications • www.superduperinc.com • 1-800-277-8737

Complete A Phrase

Directions: Complete the phrases with the correct word from the Word Bank below. Read/say the phrases aloud. Variation: Roll a die to see how many times you have to say the phrase.

1. _____ of water

2. wearing a _____

3. smelling the _____

4. sitting in a _____

5. eating a _____

6. hug and _____

7. spoon and _____

Word Bank

kiss	chair	sip	rose

shoe	fig	fork

_____   _____   _____
Name   Date   Homework Partner

Letter Shuffle

Directions: Read/say aloud the picture-words. Then, unscramble the letters in parenthesis after each phrase. (Scrambled words are the same as picture-words.) Write the word in the blank space. Read/say each phrase.

leaf

shop

1. to _____ (psoh)

2. on a _____ boat (lias)

nice

3. _____ homework (hamt)

4. _____ friend (einc)

4

four

5. fall _____ (fael)

6. one, two, three, _____ (ourf)

math

sail

Answer Key: 1. shop 2. sail 3. math 4. nice 5. leaf 6. four

_____ _____ _____

Name　　　　　　Date　　　　Homework Partner

Stopping Phrase Level

#BK-320 Webber® Photo Phonology Minimal Pair Cards Fun Sheets • ©2005 Super Duper® Publications • www.superduperinc.com • 1-800-277-8737

Fold Again

Directions: Fold this page along the dotted lines so that the arrows at the top meet. Read/say aloud the phrases you see using the describing word and the picture-word *("round **plum**")*.

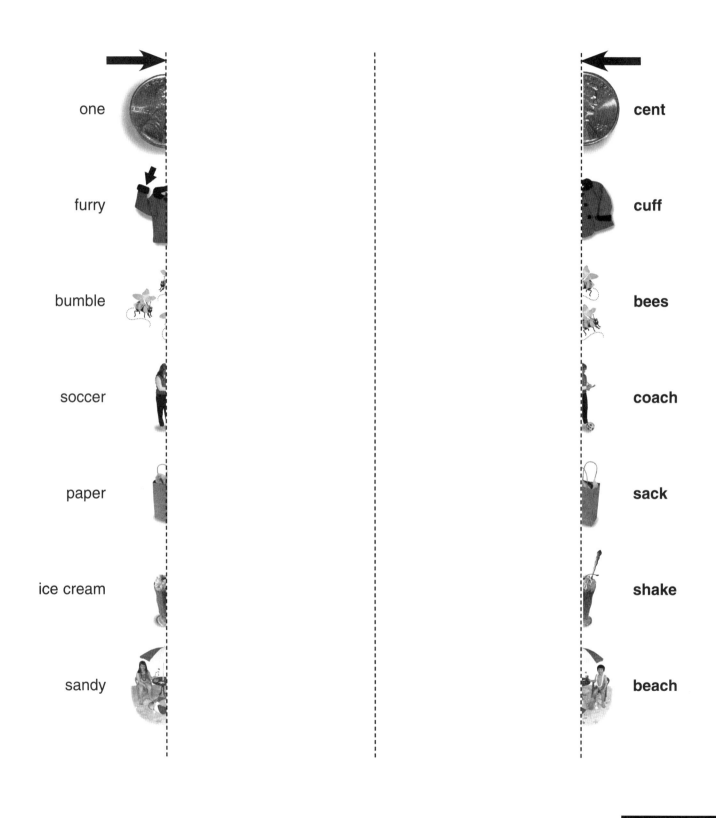

one	cent
furry	**cuff**
bumble	**bees**
soccer	**coach**
paper	**sack**
ice cream	**shake**
sandy	**beach**

_____ _____ _____

Name　　　　　　　　Date　　　　　　Homework Partner

Stopping Phrase Level

Mine or Yours?

Directions: Read/say each picture-word below. Cut out the pictures and put face down in a pile. Turn over a picture and flip a coin. Heads means you keep the picture and say, *"my _____"* *("my shape")*. Tails means you give the picture to your partner and say, *"your _____"* *("your shape")*. Most pictures at the end wins.

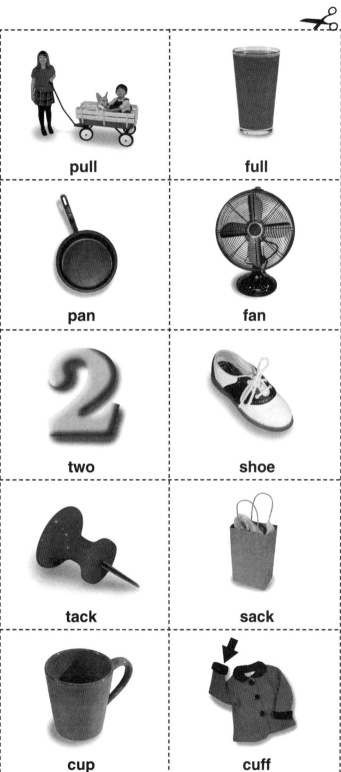

toe	sew
tape	shape
cat	cash
mitt	miss
tie	thigh
pull	full
pan	fan
two	shoe
tack	sack
cup	cuff

_____ _____ _____

Name Date Homework Partner

Stopping Phrase Level

#BK-320 Webber® Photo Phonology Minimal Pair Cards Fun Sheets • ©2005 Super Duper® Publications • www.superduperinc.com • 1-800-277-8737

"I would…"

Directions: Read/say the questions below. Answer them aloud, using the target word in a sentence.
("I would buy a vanilla shake.")

1. If you had all the you wanted, what would you buy?

   cash

2. If you went to the , what would you do?

   beach

3. If you could buy a , what flavor would you buy?

   shake

4. If you had a magic , where would it take you?

   chair

5. If you could , what would you make?

   sew

6. If you bought a , who would you give it to?

   rose

7. If you could buy new toys, what would you buy?

   four

_____   _____   _____
Name   Date   Homework Partner

Stopping Sentence Level

Silly Sentences

Directions: Read/say each sentence below. Change the underlined word in the sentence so that it makes sense using a picture-word from the Word Bank. Then, read/say the corrected sentence aloud.

Word Bank

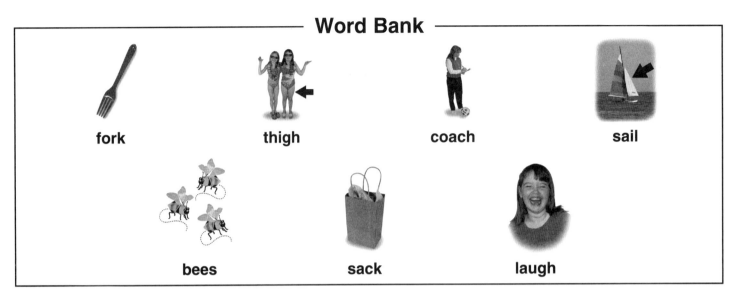

fork   thigh   coach   sail

bees   sack   laugh

1. A boat has a <u>pedal</u>.

2. <u>Cats</u> make honey.

3. Set the table with a knife, <u>crayon</u>, and spoon.

4. When something is funny, people <u>cry</u>.

5. The <u>scientist</u> and players celebrated the team's win.

6. Carry your groceries home in a paper <u>box</u>.

7. Your <u>elbow</u> is part of your leg.

Answers: 1. sail 2. bees 3. fork 4. laugh 5. coach 6. sack 7. thigh

_____   _____   _____

Name   Date   Homework Partner

Stopping Sentence Level

#BK-320 Webber® Photo Phonology Minimal Pair Cards Fun Sheets • ©2005 Super Duper® Publications • www.superduperinc.com • 1-800-277-8737

One, Two, Three

Directions: Each student gets three turns to roll the die. The number on the die corresponds to the number next to the phrase to be used in a silly sentence. For example, a student who rolls a two, five, and one will make a sentence with the phrases: *"A young woman cuts long hair and wanted to shop."*

	Roll One	Roll Two	Roll Three
	1. The little boy	bought some apples	and wanted to shop.
	2. A young woman	took a sip of water	out of the tub.
	3. The smart student	jumped rope	while doing math homework.
	4. The wild monkey	tried on a jacket	with a furry cuff.
	5. The old man	cuts long hair	with a shoe.
	6. A thrifty girl	saved every cent	to buy a puppy.

_____   _____   _____

Name   Date   Homework Partner

Spin a Sentence

Directions: Read/say aloud the picture-words below. If you prefer, glue this page to construction paper for added durability. Cut out the arrow/dial. Use a brad to connect the dial to the circle. Spin the spinner. When you land on a sentence, complete the sentence by choosing the correct picture-word. Read/say the sentence aloud.

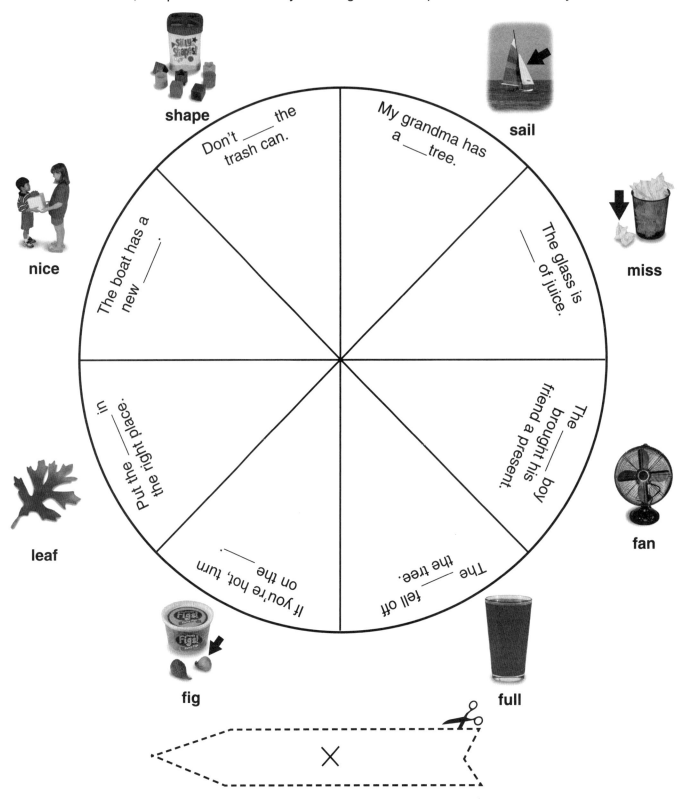

shape

sail

nice

miss

leaf

fan

fig

full

Don't _____ the trash can.

My grandma has a _____ tree.

The boat has a new _____.

The glass is _____ of juice.

Put the _____ in the right place.

The _____ brought his friend a present.

If you're hot, turn on the _____.

The _____ fell off the tree.

_____   _____   _____
Name   Date   Homework Partner

#BK-320 Webber® Photo Phonology Minimal Pair Cards Fun Sheets • ©2005 Super Duper® Publications • www.superduperinc.com • 1-800-277-8737

Auditory Bombardment

Directions: Have the student listen carefully as you read the following list of words slowly and clearly. The student does not need to repeat the words, but just listen to them. You may have the student engage in a quiet activity, like coloring, as you read.

1. spot	34. stone	67. trip
2. spout	35. stay	68. tree
3. spool	36. storm	69. trail
4. spill	37. stove	70. truck
5. space	38. snail	71. trick
6. spin	39. snack	72. drip
7. spoil	40. snake	73. dream
8. sponge	41. snoop	74. drive
9. spoon	42. snore	75. dress
10. sports	43. snow	76. crawl
11. spy	44. ski	77. crab
12. swing	45. scare	78. crib
13. sweep	46. school	79. crown
14. sweet	47. score	80. grass
15. swim	48. scout	81. grape
16. swan	49. skip	82. grow
17. sweat	50. skin	83. play
18. sway	51. skirt	84. plane
19. stop	52. sky	85. please
20. stack	53. break	86. plum
21. stool	54. bread	87. blocks
22. stain	55. braid	88. blow
23. stairs	56. brave	89. black
24. stamp	57. breathe	90. bloom
25. stand	58. bride	91. floor
26. star	59. bridge	92. fly
27. state	60. frog	93. flip
28. steak	61. free	94. floss
29. stem	62. fry	95. clap
30. step	63. fruit	96. clean
31. stew	64. freeze	97. class
32. stick	65. friend	98. glass
33. store	66. front	99. glove
		100. glow

Name   Date   Homework Partner

Cluster Reduction Word Level

Minimal Contrast Pairs

Directions: Have student point to picture-words as teacher/helper says each word aloud.

1.
pot   spot

2.
pout   spout

3.
pool   spool

4.
pill   spill

5.
wing   swing

6.
top   stop

7.
tack   stack

8.
tool   stool

9.
nail   snail

10.
key   ski

_____   _____   _____

Name   Date   Homework Partner

Minimal Contrast Pairs

Directions: Have student point to picture-words as teacher/helper says each word aloud.

1.		6.	
bake	**break**	**tail**	**trail**

2.		7.	
bed	**bread**	**dip**	**drip**

3.		8.	
fog	**frog**	**call**	**crawl**

4.		9.	
tip	**trip**	**cab**	**crab**

5.		10.	
tea	**tree**	**gas**	**grass**

_____ _____ _____

Name　　　　　　　　Date　　　　　　Homework Partner

Minimal Contrast Pairs

Directions: Have student point to picture-words as teacher/helper says each word aloud.

1.

pay   play

2.

pain   plane

3.

box   blocks

4.

bow   blow

5.

four   floor

6.

cap   clap

7.

gas   glass

8.

go   glow

9.

tool   stool

10.

top   stop

_____   _____   _____
Name   Date   Homework Partner

#BK-320 Webber® Photo Phonology Minimal Pair Cards Fun Sheets • ©2005 Super Duper® Publications • www.superduperinc.com • 1-800-277-8737

Minimal Contrast Definitions

Directions: Read each question and possible answers aloud. Ask students to circle and/or say the correct answer.

1. What is used for planting flowers?

pot   **spot**

2. What is another name for a dot on a dog?

pot   **spot**

3. What is part of a pitcher?

pout   **spout**

4. What do you do when you don't get what you want?

pout   **spout**

5. What holds thread?

pool   **spool**

6. Where can you swim?

pool   **spool**

7. What is medicine that you swallow whole?

pill   **spill**

8. What happens when you turn your drink over?

pill   **spill**

9. Which one is a part of a bird?

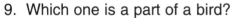

wing   **swing**

10. What do you do on the playground?

wing   **swing**

_____ _____ _____

Name   Date   Homework Partner

Cluster Reduction Word Level

Minimal Contrast Definitions

Directions: Read each question and possible answers aloud. Ask students to circle and/or say the correct answer.

1. Which one is a toy?

    top   **stop**

2. What does a red light or sign mean?

    top   **stop**

3. What do you do with blocks?

    tack   **stack**

4. What holds paper on a cork board?

    tack   **stack**

5. What do you use for sitting?

    tool   **stool**

6. What is a wrench?

    tool   **stool**

7. What animal crawls slowly?

    nail   **snail**

8. What do you hit with a hammer?

    nail   **snail**

9. What opens a door?

    key   **ski**

10. What sport do you do on snow?

    key   **ski**

_____   _____   _____

Name   Date   Homework Partner

Cluster Reduction Word Level

#BK-320 Webber® Photo Phonology Minimal Pair Cards Fun Sheets • ©2005 Super Duper® Publications • www.superduperinc.com • 1-800-277-8737

Minimal Contrast Definitions

Directions: Read each question and possible answers aloud. Ask students to circle and/or say the correct answer.

1. What do you do with cookie dough?

bake   **break**

2. What is another way to crack an egg?

bake   **break**

3. What food makes a sandwich?

bed   **bread**

4. What do you use for sleeping?

bed   **bread**

5. What does a heavy mist look like?

fog   **frog**

6. What animal says "ribbit"?

fog   **frog**

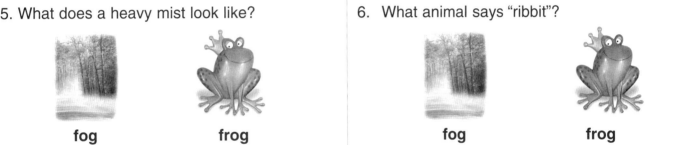

7. When you go on vacation, you go on a...

tip   **trip**

8. What is another name for the point of a crayon?

tip   **trip**

9. Which one is a drink?

tea   **tree**

10. What do you find in a forest?

tea   **tree**

_____ _____ _____

Name   Date   Homework Partner

Cluster Reduction Word Level

Minimal Contrast Definitions

Directions: Read each question and possible answers aloud. Ask students to circle and/or say the correct answer.

1. What is another name for a path?

tail   **trail**

2. What does a cat wag?

tail   **trail**

3. What do you put on chips?

dip   **drip**

4. What does ice cream do when it melts?

dip   **drip**

5. What does a baby do?

call   **crawl**

6. You dial a phone to make a...

call   **crawl**

7. What do you ride in the city?

cab   **crab**

8. What animal has pincers?

cab   **crab**

9. What grows on a lawn?

gas   **grass**

10. What does a car need to run?

gas   **grass**

_____ _____ _____

Name   Date   Homework Partner

Cluster Reduction Word Level

#BK-320 Webber® Photo Phonology Minimal Pair Cards Fun Sheets • ©2005 Super Duper® Publications • www.superduperinc.com • 1-800-277-8737

Minimal Contrast Definitions

Directions: Read each question and possible answers aloud. Ask students to circle and/or say the correct answer.

1. When you buy something you must...

pay　　**play**

2. What do children do with toys?

pay　　**play**

3. What do you feel when you are hurt?

pain　　**plane**

4. What flies?

pain　　**plane**

5. What do you use to mail packages?

box　　**blocks**

6. What can you stack?

box　　**blocks**

7. What do you do to a whistle?

bow　　**blow**

8. What do you put on a gift?

bow　　**blow**

9. Which one is a number?

four　　**floor**

10. What do you walk on?

four　　**floor**

_____ _____ _____

Name　　　　　Date　　　　　Homework Partner

Minimal Contrast Definitions

Directions: Read each question and possible answers aloud. Ask students to circle and/or say the correct answer.

1. What do you wear on your head?

cap **clap**

2. What do you do with your hands?

cap **clap**

3. What do you use for drinking?

gas **glass**

4. What is another name for fuel?

gas **glass**

5. What does a green light mean?

go **glow**

6. What does a jack-o'-lantern do in the dark?

go **glow**

7. What animal says "ribbit"?

fog **frog**

8. What does a heavy mist look like?

fog **frog**

9. What does a car need to run?

gas **grass**

10. What makes a lawn?

gas **grass**

_____ _____ _____

Name Date Homework Partner

Cluster Reduction Word Level

#BK-320 Webber® Photo Phonology Minimal Pair Cards Fun Sheets • ©2005 Super Duper® Publications • www.superduperinc.com • 1-800-277-8737

Friendly Frog

Directions: Cut out the flies below and place them in a pile. Then, cut along the dotted line to make the frog's mouth. Draw a card and read/say the picture-word aloud as you feed the frog.

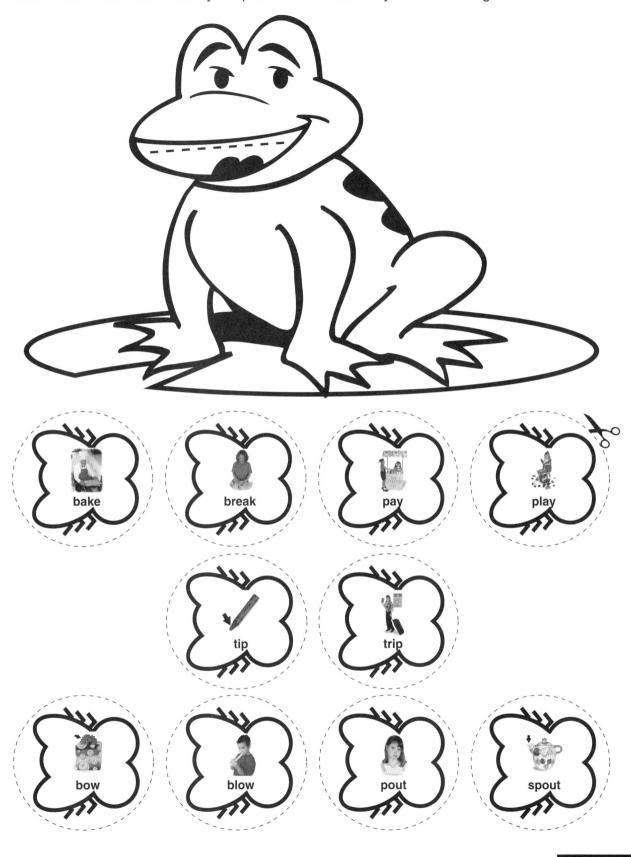

bake

break

pay

play

tip

trip

bow

blow

pout

spout

_____ _____ _____

Name   Date   Homework Partner

Memory Game

Directions: Read/say aloud each picture-word below. Cut out the pictures. Place all cards face down. Turn over cards two at a time and try to find a match. Say each card as you pick it up. Keep all matches. Most matches wins!

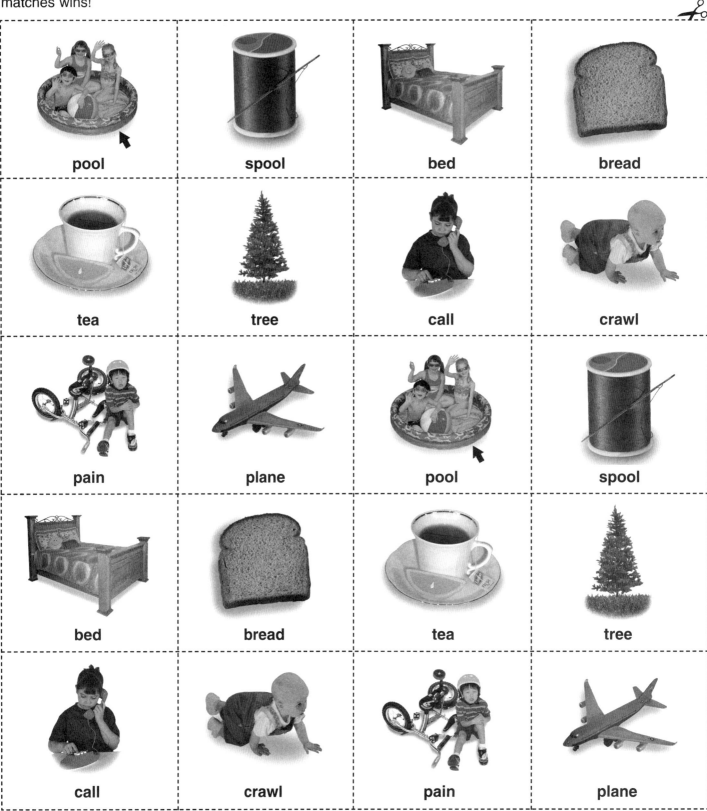

pool	spool	bed	bread
tea	tree	call	crawl
pain	plane	pool	spool
bed	bread	tea	tree
call	crawl	pain	plane

_____ _____ _____
Name   Date   Homework Partner

#BK-320 Webber® Photo Phonology Minimal Pair Cards Fun Sheets • ©2005 Super Duper® Publications • www.superduperinc.com • 1-800-277-8737

Hide 'n' Seek

Directions: Read/say aloud the picture-words. Cut out the pictures and penny. Place the pictures face up. Teacher/helper hides the penny under a picture. Say each picture-word as you look underneath for the penny. Find the penny and you win!

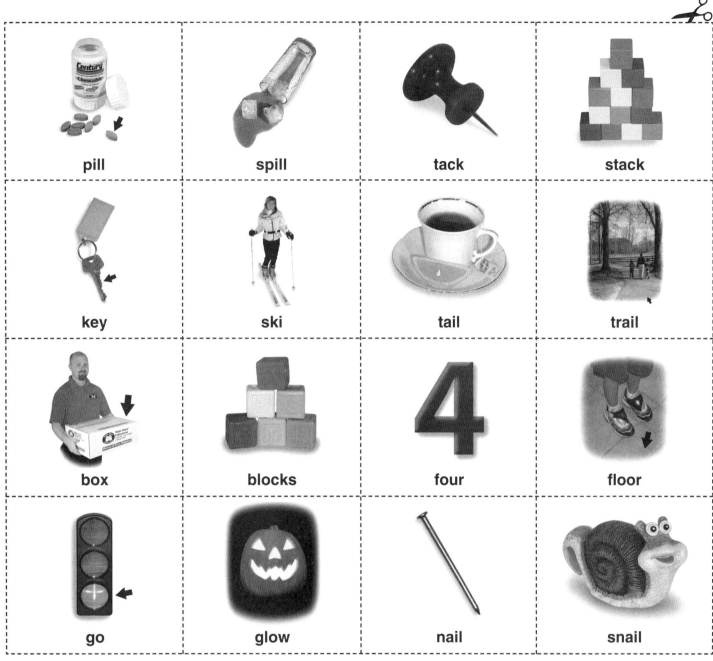

pill	spill	tack	stack
key	ski	tail	trail
box	blocks	four	floor
go	glow	nail	snail

_____ _____ _____

Name   Date   Homework Partner

Cluster Reduction Word Level

Slide and Say

Directions: Read/say aloud the picture-words below. Then, cut out all the cards. "Slide" the cards down the slide, reading/saying each word aloud as you slide.

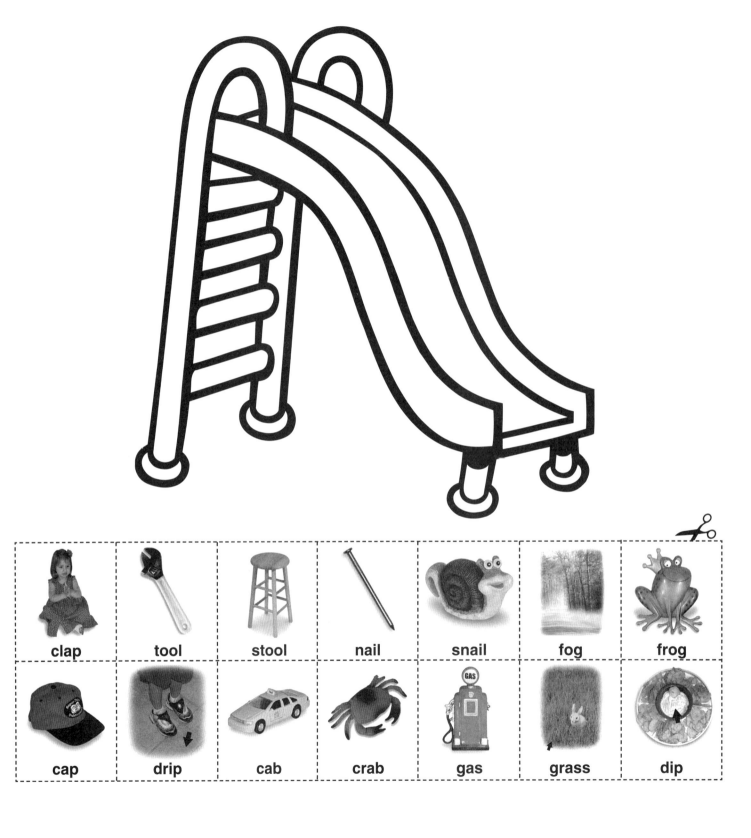

clap	tool	stool	nail	snail	fog	frog
cap	drip	cab	crab	gas	grass	dip

#BK-320 Webber® Photo Phonology Minimal Pair Cards Fun Sheets • ©2005 Super Duper® Publications • www.superduperinc.com • 1-800-277-8737

_____ _____ _____
Name   Date   Homework Partner

X and O

Directions: Cut out each X and O below. Have each player/partner choose X or O. The first player reads/says a picture-phrase aloud and places an X or O on the square. Play continues in turn. The first person to get three in a row wins.

spool of thread	clapping your hands	a fir tree
to swing outside	a bull frog	stack of blocks
blowing the whistle	taking a trip	a black spot

_____ _____ _____

Name   Date   Homework Partner

Cluster Reduction Phrase Level

#BK-320 Webber® Photo Phonology Minimal Pair Cards Fun Sheets • ©2005 Super Duper® Publications • www.superduperinc.com • 1-800-277-8737

81

Letter Shuffle

Directions: Read/say aloud the picture-words. Then, unscramble the letters in parenthesis after each phrase. (Scrambled words are the same as picture-words.) Write the word in the blank space. Read/say each phrase.

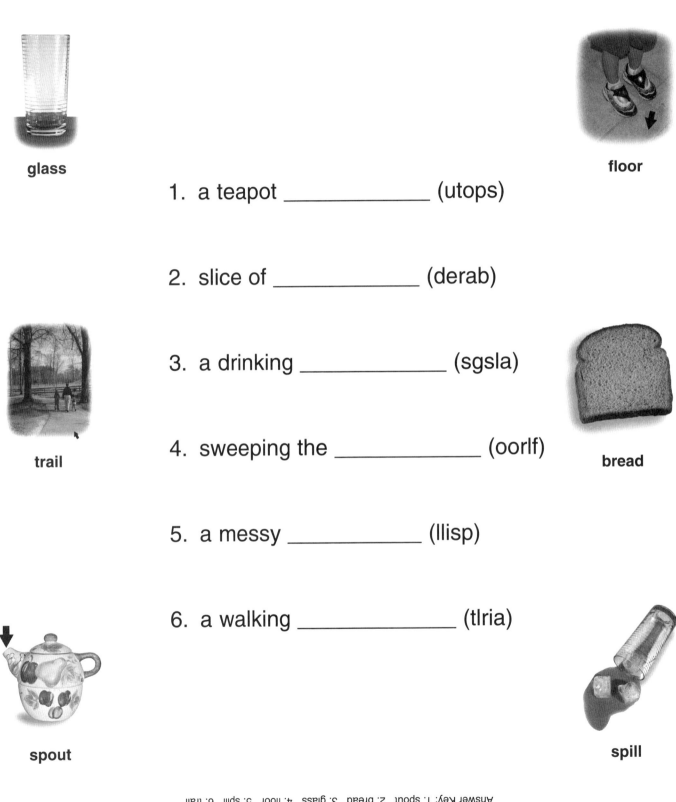

glass

floor

1. a teapot _____ (utops)

2. slice of _____ (derab)

3. a drinking _____ (sgsla)

4. sweeping the _____ (oorlf)

trail

bread

5. a messy _____ (llisp)

6. a walking _____ (tlria)

spout

spill

Answer Key: 1. spout 2. bread 3. glass 4. floor 5. spill 6. trail

_____ _____ _____

Name   Date   Homework Partner

#BK-320 Webber® Photo Phonology Minimal Pair Cards Fun Sheets • ©2005 Super Duper® Publications • www.superduperinc.com • 1-800-277-8737

Puzzle Match

Directions: Draw a line from a puzzle piece in Column A to the one that matches it in Column B. Read/say the completed phrases aloud.

A

B

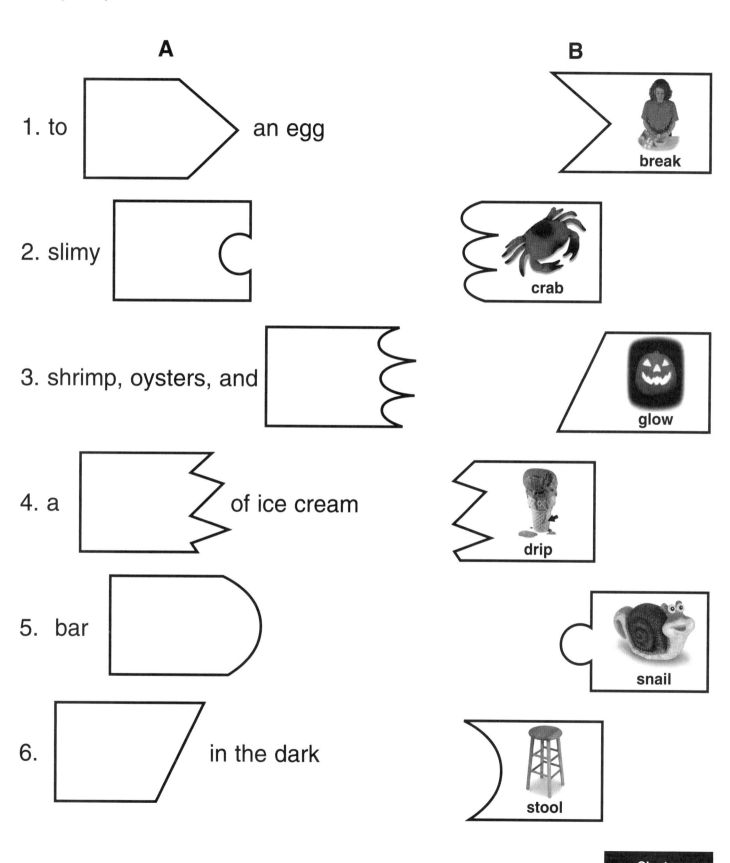

1. to   an egg

break

2. slimy

crab

3. shrimp, oysters, and

glow

4. a   of ice cream

drip

5. bar

snail

6.   in the dark

stool

Name   Date   Homework Partner

#BK-320 Webber® Photo Phonology Minimal Pair Cards Fun Sheets • ©2005 Super Duper® Publications • www.superduperinc.com • 1-800-277-8737

Fix It! Phrases

Directions: Each phrase below has an underlined incorrect letter in it. Fix each phrase by saying/circling the correct letter on the right side of the book. Read/say aloud each correct phrase.

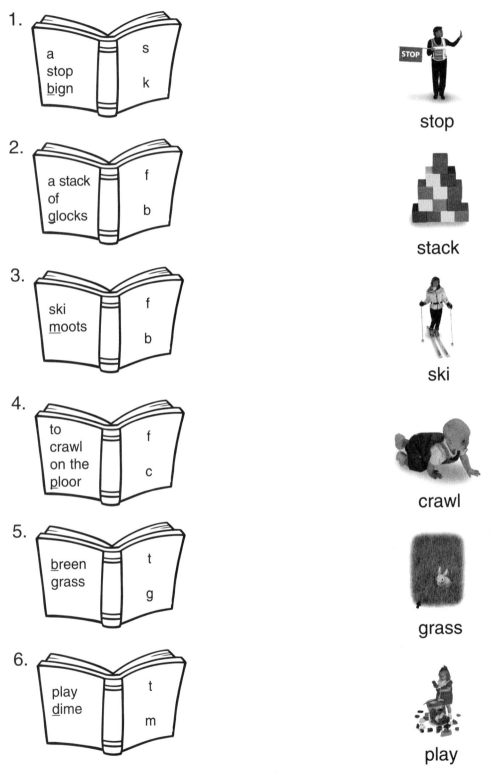

1. a stop <u>b</u>ign   s   k

stop

2. a stack of <u>g</u>locks   f   b

stack

3. ski <u>m</u>oots   f   b

ski

4. to crawl on the <u>p</u>loor   f   c

crawl

5. <u>b</u>reen grass   t   g

grass

6. play <u>d</u>ime   t   m

play

Answer key: 1. s 2. b 3. b 4. f 5. g 6. t

_____ _____ _____

Name   Date   Homework Partner

Cluster Reduction Phrase Level

Sentence Fill-In

Directions: Draw a line from the sentence in Column A to the picture-word that completes it in Column B.

A

1. _____ for the winner.

2. Let's go on a _____.

3. The Dalmatian has more than one _____.

4. Stack the _____.

5. Sit on a _____.

6. The baby likes to _____ on the floor.

7. _____ on the playground.

B

crawl

stool

swing

trip

clap

spot

blocks

_____ _____ _____
Name   Date   Homework Partner

Which One?

Directions: Read/say each picture-word on the right. Then, answer each question by circling the correct answer. Read/say each answer aloud using a complete sentence.

1. Which one crawls?

    snail   frog

2. Which one swims?

    tool   crab

3. Which one breaks?

    spot   glass

4. Which one hops?

    frog   wing

5. Which one flies?

    bed   plane

6. Which one grows?

    tree   pool

7. Which one is a sport?

    ski   bread

Answer key: 1. snail 2. crab 3. glass 4. frog 5. plane 6. tree 7. ski

_____   _____   _____

Name   Date   Homework Partner

#BK-320 Webber® Photo Phonology Minimal Pair Cards Fun Sheets • ©2005 Super Duper® Publications • www.superduperinc.com • 1-800-277-8737

At the Market

Directions: Read/say each picture-word on the shelves. Cut out the $1 bills below. Give a dollar bill to your homework partner as you pick out something to buy. Say, *"I want to buy (a) _____ ."*

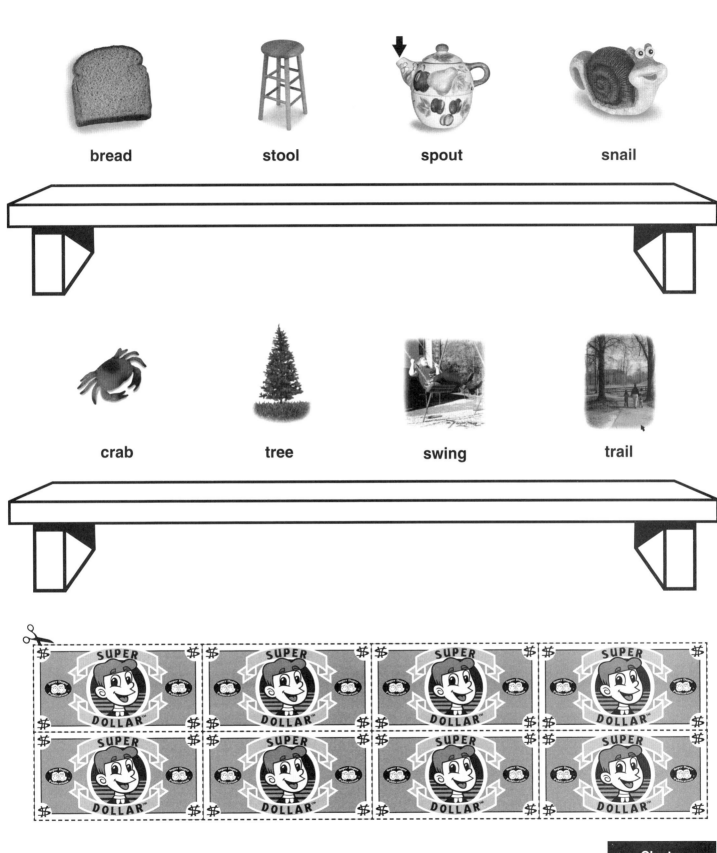

bread   stool   spout   snail

crab   tree   swing   trail

_____   _____   _____
Name   Date   Homework Partner

Cluster Reduction Sentence Level

Story Loop

Directions: Read/say aloud each picture-word. Make up a story using all of the pictures in the circle. You can start anywhere in the circle and go in either direction, but you must always end where you started to complete the loop.

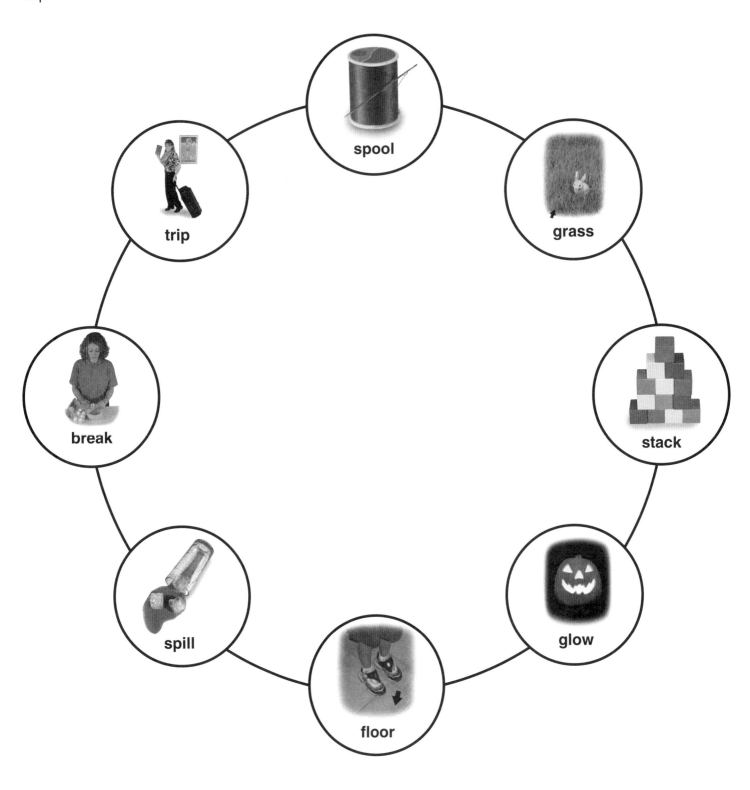

_____ _____ _____

Name   Date   Homework Partner

#BK-320 Webber® Photo Phonology Minimal Pair Cards Fun Sheets • ©2005 Super Duper® Publications • www.superduperinc.com • 1-800-277-8737

Auditory Bombardment

Directions: Have the student listen carefully as you read the following list of words slowly and clearly. The student does not need to repeat the words, but just listen to them. You may have the student engage in a quiet activity, like coloring, as you read.

1. farm	34. off	67. change
2. fin	35. shell	68. charm
3. four	36. shoe	69. cheek
4. fold	37. show	70. chest
5. file	38. shape	71. child
6. fig	39. shark	72. chin
7. face	40. sharp	73. chip
8. fall	41. shawl	74. chop
9. fan	42. shed	75. chore
10. far	43. sheep	76. hatch
11. fast	44. sheet	77. beach
12. fat	45. shelf	78. teach
13. fear	46. shield	79. bench
14. feel	47. shine	80. coach
15. fence	48 ship	81. ditch
16. fish	49. shirt	82. peach
17. foot	50. shop	83. speech
18. fork	51. shout	84. castle
19. phone	52. shut	85. ace
20. beef	53. cash	86. moose
21. cliff	54. brush	87. goose
22. calf	55. fish	88. race
23. cough	56. fresh	89. price
24. half	57. leash	90. bows
25. knife	58. mash	91. rose
26. laugh	59. squash	92. eyes
27. leaf	60. trash	93. knees
28. rough	61. wash	94. fries
29. stuff	62. wish	95. cage
30. thief	63. cheer	96. wedge
31. tough	64. cheese	97. judge
32. wife	65. chalk	98. bridge
33. wolf	66. chair	99. page
		100. pledge

Name   Date   Homework Partner

Stridency Deletion Word Level

Minimal Contrast Pairs

Directions: Have student point to picture-words as teacher/helper says each word aloud.

1.
arm   farm

2.
in   fin

3.
oar   four

4.
old   fold

5.
pile   file

6.
pig   fig

7.
bee   beef

8.
clip   cliff

9.
cap   calf

10.
talk   chalk

_____ _____ _____
Name   Date   Homework Partner

**Stridency
Deletion
Word Level**

#BK-320 Webber® Photo Phonology Minimal Pair Cards Fun Sheets • ©2005 Super Duper® Publications • www.superduperinc.com • 1-800-277-8737

Minimal Contrast Pairs

Directions: Have student point to picture-words as teacher/helper says each word aloud.

1. L   shell

2. two   shoe

3. toe   show

4. tape   shape

5. eat   sheet

6. cat   cash

7. ear   cheer

8. tees   cheese

9. talk   chalk

10. bow   bows

_____ _____ _____

Name   Date   Homework Partner

Stridency Deletion Word Level

Minimal Contrast Pairs

Directions: Have student point to picture-words as teacher/helper says each word aloud.

1.

hat   hatch

2.

beet   beach

3.

tea   teach

4.

cattle   castle

5.

eight   ace

6.

Moo

moo   moose

7.

bow   bows

8.

row   rose

9.

eye   eyes

10.

K   cage

Name _____ Date _____ Homework Partner _____

Stridency Deletion Word Level

#BK-320 Webber® Photo Phonology Minimal Pair Cards Fun Sheets • ©2005 Super Duper® Publications • www.superduperinc.com • 1-800-277-8737

Minimal Contrast Definitions

Directions: Read each question and possible answers aloud. Ask students to circle and/or say the correct answer.

1. Which one is a body part?

arm **farm**

2. Where do pigs, cows, and horses live?

arm **farm**

3. What is part of a fish?

in **fin**

4. What is the opposite of "out"?

in **fin**

5. What do you use to paddle?

oar **four**

6. Which one is a number?

oar **four**

7. What is the opposite of "new"?

old **fold**

8. What do you do with clean towels?

old **fold**

9. What is another name for a folder?

pile **file**

10. What is a stack of clothes called?

pile **file**

_____ _____ _____

Name   Date   Homework Partner

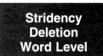

Stridency Deletion Word Level

Minimal Contrast Definitions

Directions: Read each question and possible answers aloud. Ask students to circle and/or say the correct answer.

1. Which one is a farm animal?

   pig   **fig**

2. Which one is a fruit?

   pig   **fig**

3. What insect buzzes and makes honey?

   bee   **beef**

4. Which one do you eat?

   bee   **beef**

5. Hold paper together with a paper...

   clip   **cliff**

6. What is the edge of a mountain called?

   clip   **cliff**

7. What has a bill?

   cap   **calf**

8. What is a baby cow called?

   cap   **calf**

9. What do you find on the beach?

   L   **shell**

10. Which one is a letter?

    L   **shell**

_____ _____ _____
Name   Date   Homework Partner

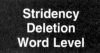

Stridency
Deletion
Word Level

#BK-320 Webber® Photo Phonology Minimal Pair Cards Fun Sheets • ©2005 Super Duper® Publications • www.superduperinc.com • 1-800-277-8737

Minimal Contrast Definitions

Directions: Read each question and possible answers aloud. Ask students to circle and/or say the correct answer.

1. Which one is a number?

   two   shoe

2. What has laces?

   two   shoe

3. What do you do when you let people see something?

   toe   show

4. What body part is on your feet?

   toe   show

5. What can you use to hold things together?

   tape   shape

6. What is a square?

   tape   shape

7. What do you do to food?

   eat   sheet

8. What do you wear to look like a ghost?

   eat   sheet

9. What animal purrs?

   cat   cash

10. What is money called?

   cat   cash

_____   _____   _____
Name   Date   Homework Partner

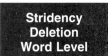

Stridency Deletion Word Level

#BK-320 Webber® Photo Phonology Minimal Pair Cards Fun Sheets • ©2005 Super Duper® Publications • www.superduperinc.com • 1-800-277-8737

Minimal Contrast Definitions

Directions: Read each question and possible answers aloud. Ask students to circle and/or say the correct answer.

1. What does a cheerleader do?

ear cheer

2. What body part hears?

ear cheer

3. What do you eat?

tees cheese

4. What do you use to play golf?

tees cheese

5. What do you use to write on a chalkboard?

talk chalk

6. What do people do with their mouths?

talk chalk

7. What do you wear on your head?

hat hatch

8. What does a baby chick do?

hat hatch

9. Where do you play in the sand?

beet beach

10. What is a vegetable?

beet beach

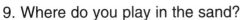

Name Date Homework Partner

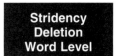

Stridency Deletion Word Level

#BK-320 Webber® Photo Phonology Minimal Pair Cards Fun Sheets • ©2005 Super Duper® Publications • www.superduperinc.com • 1-800-277-8737

Minimal Contrast Definitions

Directions: Read each question and possible answers aloud. Ask students to circle and/or say the correct answer.

1. What drink can be served hot or cold?

tea   **teach**

2. What does a teacher do?

tea   **teach**

3. Where does a king live?

cattle   **castle**

4. What do you call many cows?

cattle   **castle**

5. Which one is a number?

eight   **ace**

6. Which one is a playing card?

eight   **ace**

7. What does a cow say?

moo   **moose**

8. What animal has a rack of horns?

moo   **moose**

9. After wrapping a present, you can put on a...

bow   **bows**

10. On your birthday, you see lots of...

bow   **bows**

_____ _____ _____

Name   Date   Homework Partner

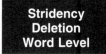

Stridency Deletion Word Level

Minimal Contrast Definitions

Directions: Read each question and possible answers aloud. Ask students to circle and/or say the correct answer.

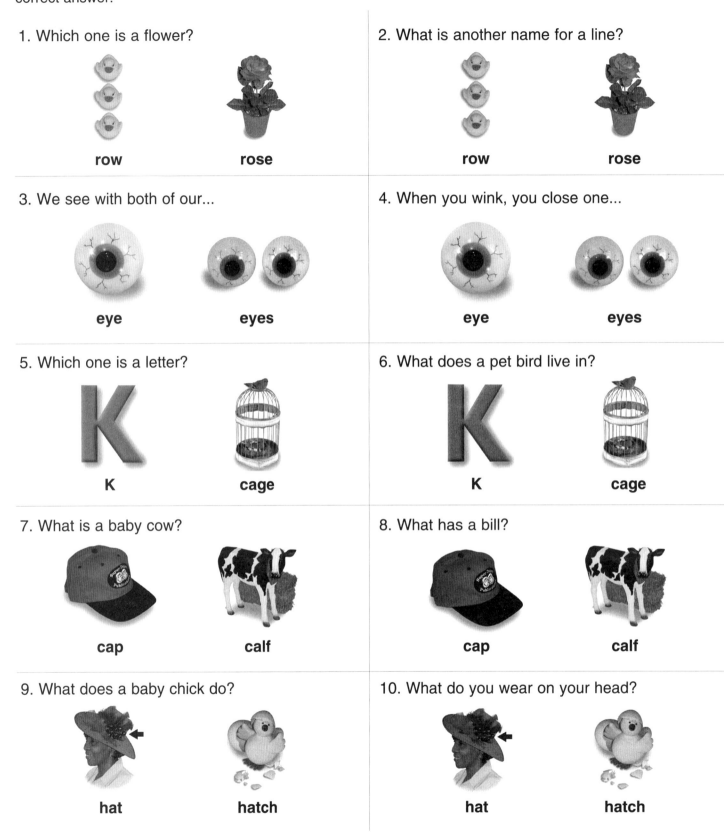

1. Which one is a flower?

row   rose

2. What is another name for a line?

row   rose

3. We see with both of our...

eye   eyes

4. When you wink, you close one...

eye   eyes

5. Which one is a letter?

K   cage

6. What does a pet bird live in?

K   cage

7. What is a baby cow?

cap   calf

8. What has a bill?

cap   calf

9. What does a baby chick do?

hat   hatch

10. What do you wear on your head?

hat   hatch

_____   _____   _____
Name   Date   Homework Partner

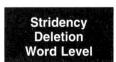

Stridency Deletion Word Level

#BK-320 Webber® Photo Phonology Minimal Pair Cards Fun Sheets • ©2005 Super Duper® Publications • www.superduperinc.com • 1-800-277-8737

Ice Cream Scoops

Directions: Read/say aloud the picture-words below. Then, cut out the ice cream cones and scoop cards. Each player gets a cone. The first player reads/says the picture-word on a scoop card and places it on his/her cone. Play continues in turn.

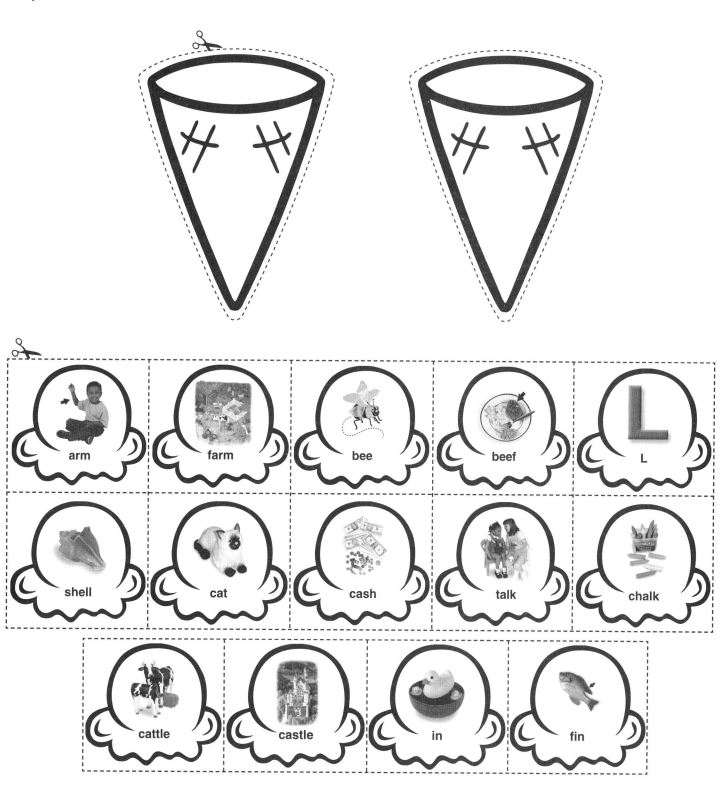

arm

farm

bee

beef

L

shell

cat

cash

talk

chalk

cattle

castle

in

fin

Name

Date

Homework Partner

Memory Game

Directions: Read/say aloud each picture-word below. Cut out the pictures. Place all cards face down. Turn over cards two at a time and try to find a match. Say each card as you pick it up. Keep all matches. Most matches wins!

eye	eyes	K	cage
ear	cheer	cap	calf
tea	teach	eye	eyes
K	cage	ear	cheer
cap	calf	tea	teach

_____ _____ _____

Name   Date   Homework Partner

#BK-320 Webber® Photo Phonology Minimal Pair Cards Fun Sheets • ©2005 Super Duper® Publications • www.superduperinc.com • 1-800-277-8737

Cheers for the Jester

Directions: Read/say aloud the picture-words below. Then, cut out the markers. Flip a coin (heads=1, tails=2) to determine how many spaces to move. As you move, read/say each picture-word aloud. First player to reach the finish wins.

eat

sheet

8 eight

rose

ace

row

pig

fold

fig

old

beet

2 two

Start

Finish

beach

shoe

_____   _____   _____
Name   Date   Homework Partner

Jars of Fun

Directions: Cut out the jelly beans below and place them face down in a pile. As you choose a jelly bean, read/say aloud the picture-word on it and glue, tape, or place the jelly bean onto the jar.

oar	four	pile	file	clip	cliff	toe
show	tees	cheese	hat	hatch	moo	moose

Name _____ Date _____ Homework Partner _____

#BK-320 Webber® Photo Phonology Minimal Pair Cards Fun Sheets • ©2005 Super Duper® Publications • www.superduperinc.com • 1-800-277-8737

Answer It!

Directions: Read each question below and choose the phrase that best answers the question. Put an X beside the correct answer. Read/say the phrases aloud.

1. What do we put on our foot?

_____ a) a sock and shoe

_____ b) a pair of earrings

2. Which one is a bird's home?

_____ a) a little cage

_____ b) busy beehive

3. What do mice eat?

_____ a) crunch dog food

_____ b) a piece of cheese

4. Which one is a big home?

_____ a) a new apartment

_____ b) an old castle

5. What is a triangle?

_____ a) a shape

_____ b) an animal

6. What number comes between 3 and 5?

_____ a) number 9

_____ b) number 4

7. What do we eat?

_____ a) wet grass

_____ b) roast beef

Answer Key: 1.a 2.a 3.b 4.b 5.a 6.b 7.b

_____ _____ _____

Name   Date   Homework Partner

Stridency Deletion Phrase Level

Letter Shuffle

Directions: Read/say aloud the picture-words. Then, unscramble the letters in parenthesis after each phrase. (Scrambled words are the same as picture-words.) Write the word in the blank space. Read/ say each phrase.

calf

fin

1. a fish _____ (nfi)

2. two blue _____ (syee)

3. a baby_____ (facl)

bows

sheet

4. a present with _____ (wosb)

5. a white _____ (tseeh)

6. the sandy _____ (hceab)

eyes

beach

Answer Key: 1. fin 2. eyes 3. calf 4. bows 5. sheet 6. beach

_____ _____ _____

Name   Date   Homework Partner

104   #BK-320 Webber® Photo Phonology Minimal Pair Cards Fun Sheets • ©2005 Super Duper® Publications • www.superduperinc.com • 1-800-277-8737

Stridency Deletion Phrase Level

Shape Match

Directions: Draw a line from a shape in Column A to the one that matches it in Column B. Read/say the phrases aloud.

A

B

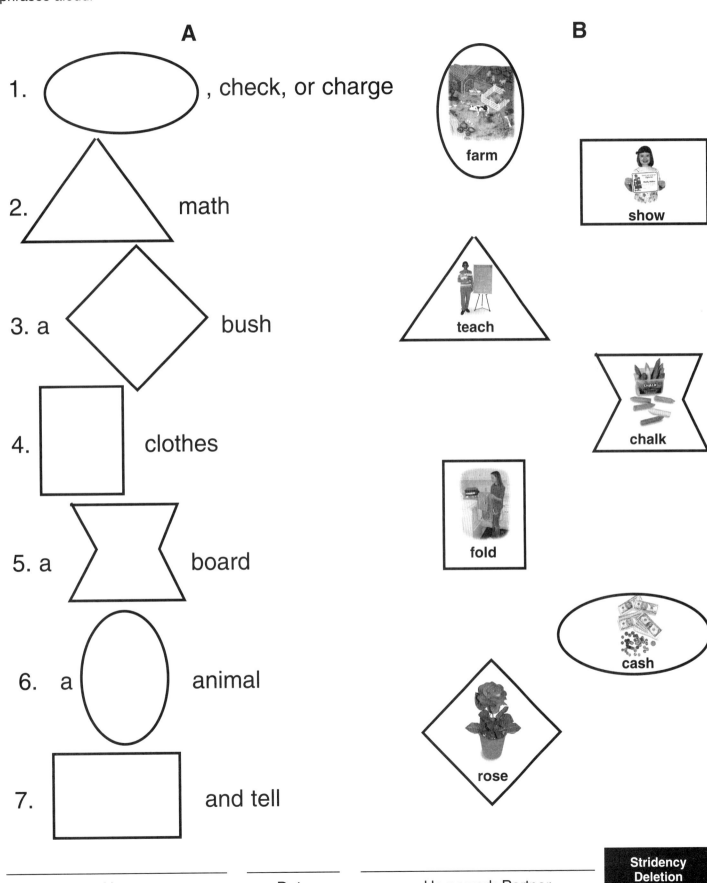

1. ⬭ , check, or charge

2. △ math

3. a ◇ bush

4. ▭ clothes

5. a ⧖ board

6. a ⬭ animal

7. ▭ and tell

farm

show

teach

chalk

fold

cash

rose

_____ _____ _____
Name   Date   Homework Partner

Stridency Deletion Phrase Level

Mine or Yours?

Directions: Read/say each picture-word below. Cut out the pictures and put face down in a pile. Turn over a picture and flip a coin. Heads means you keep the picture and say, *"my _____"* (*"my shell"*). Tails means you give the picture to your partner and say, *"your _____"* (*"your shell"*). Most pictures at the end wins!

file	fig
cliff	shell
hatch	ace
moose	four
cage	chalk

_____ _____ _____
Name   Date   Homework Partner

#BK-320 Webber® Photo Phonology Minimal Pair Cards Fun Sheets • ©2005 Super Duper® Publications • www.superduperinc.com • 1-800-277-8737

Which One?

Directions: Read/say each picture-word on the right. Then, answer each question by circling the correct answer. Read/say each answer aloud using a complete sentence.

A   **B**

1. Which one sees?

   eyes   arm

2. Which one writes?

   tape   chalk

3. Which one moos?

   cat   calf

4. Which one walks?

   moose   bee

5. Which one holds papers?

   shell   file

6. Which one buys things?

   cash   oar

7. Which one is a fruit?

   tea   fig

Answer key: 1. eyes 2. chalk 3. calf 4. moose 5. file 6. cash 7. fig

Name _____ Date _____ Homework Partner _____

Replace It

Directions: Read/say each sentence below. Change the underlined word in the sentence so that it makes sense using a picture-word from the Word Bank. Then, read/say the corrected sentence aloud.

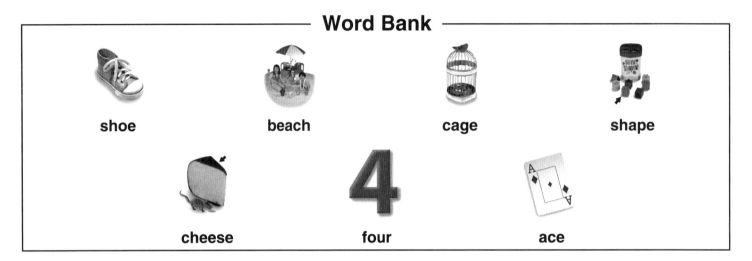

Word Bank

shoe   beach   cage   shape

cheese   four   ace

1. A parrot lives in a <u>cave</u>.

2. <u>Z</u> is a number.

3. You wear a <u>curtain</u>.

4. A square is a <u>food</u>.

5. You can eat <u>pants</u>.

6. An <u>igloo</u> is a card.

7. Play in the sand at the <u>mall</u>.

Answer Key: 1. cage 2. four 3. shoe 4. shape 5. cheese 6. ace 7. beach

#BK-320 Webber® Photo Phonology Minimal Pair Cards Fun Sheets • ©2005 Super Duper® Publications • www.superduperinc.com • 1-800-277-8737

One, Two, Three

Directions: Each student gets three turns to roll the die. The number on the die corresponds to the number next to the phrase to be used in a silly sentence. For example, a student who rolls a two, five, and one will make a sentence with the phrases: *"The old man finds a magic shell in the garden."*

	Roll One	**Roll Two**	**Roll Three**
1.	The gardener	waters the rose	in the garden.
2.	The old man	likes to eat beef	in the kitchen.
3.	The farmer	watches the chicks	as they hatch.
4.	A little pig	eats cottage cheese	on the farm.
5.	The child	finds a magic shell	at the beach.
6.	The young woman	likes to teach math	at school.

_____   _____   _____

Name   Date   Homework Partner

Scrambled Sentences

Directions: Unscramble each sentence and write it on the line below the egg. Then, read/say the sentence aloud.

1. _____

_____ .

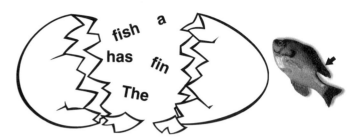

2. _____

_____ .

3. _____

_____ .

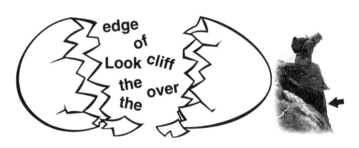

4. _____

_____ .

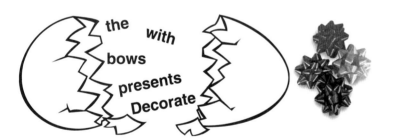

5. _____

_____ .

6. _____

_____ .

Answer Key:

1. The queen and king live in a castle.
2. The fish has a fin.
3. Please show us your award.
4. Look over the edge of the cliff.
5. Decorate the presents with bows.
6. Fold the clothes in the dryer.

_____ _____ _____
Name   Date   Homework Partner

#BK-320 Webber® Photo Phonology Minimal Pair Cards Fun Sheets • ©2005 Super Duper® Publications • www.superduperinc.com • 1-800-277-8737

Auditory Bombardment

Directions: Have the student listen carefully as you read the following list of words slowly and clearly. The student does not need to repeat the words, but just listen to them. You may have the student engage in a quiet activity, like coloring, as you read.

1. ripe	34. rust	67. luck
2. rail	35. rope	68. lamb
3. rock	36. roof	69. lawn
4. rag	37. rug	70. lace
5. read	38. round	71. lime
6. red	39. rule	72. lap
7. rain	40. roll	73. love
8. rich	41. rub	74. lake
9. run	42. crack	75. lung
10. rest	43. creek	76. land
11. ring	44. crumb	77. line
12. reel	45. crisp	78. large
13. write	46. crust	79. laugh
14. rake	47. crib	80. late
15. race	48. grin	81. league
16. ride	49. graze	82. learn
17. ranch	50. green	83. leave
18. rip	51. grip	84. listen
19. rose	52. grease	85. log
20. robe	53. groom	86. loud
21. rice	54. treat	87. lunch
22. rib	55. track	88. light
23. roast	56. trace	89. left
24. rough	57. troops	90. lid
25. row	58. trip	91. lift
26. role	59. trust	92. lead
27. root	60. leak	93. law
28. rye	61. lick	94. lamp
29. wrist	62. lip	95. latch
30. wrong	63. lay	96. clean
31. wreath	64. leap	97. clear
32. wrap	65. Lynn	98. close
33. rush	66. lizard	99. clip
		100. climb

Gliding Word Level

_____   _____   _____
Name   Date   Homework Partner

#BK-320 Webber® Photo Phonology Minimal Pair Cards Fun Sheets • ©2005 Super Duper® Publications • www.superduperinc.com • 1-800-277-8737

Minimal Contrast Pairs

Directions: Have student point to picture-words as teacher/helper says each word aloud.

1.
wipe   ripe

2.
whale   rail

3.
wok   rock

4.
wag   rag

5.
weed   read

6.
wed   red

7.
Wayne   rain

8.
witch   rich

9.
one   run

10.
west   rest

Name   Date   Homework Partner

#BK-320 Webber® Photo Phonology Minimal Pair Cards Fun Sheets • ©2005 Super Duper® Publications • www.superduperinc.com • 1-800-277-8737

Minimal Contrast Pairs

Directions: Have student point to picture-words as teacher/helper says each word aloud.

1. wing / ring

2. wheel / reel

3. white / write

4. wake / rake

5. weed / read

6. whip / lip

7. weigh / lay

8. weep / leap

9. week / leak

10. wick / lick

_____ _____ _____

Name   Date   Homework Partner

Gliding Word Level

Minimal Contrast Pairs

Directions: Have student point to picture-words as teacher/helper says each word aloud.

1. win — Lynn
2. wizard — lizard
3. yuck — luck
4. yam — lamb
5. yawn — lawn
6. quack — crack
7. Gwen — grin
8. tweet — treat
9. queen — clean
10. one — run

_____ _____ _____

Name   Date   Homework Partner

Gliding Word Level

#BK-320 Webber® Photo Phonology Minimal Pair Cards Fun Sheets • ©2005 Super Duper® Publications • www.superduperinc.com • 1-800-277-8737

Minimal Contrast Definitions

Directions: Read each question and possible answers aloud. Ask students to circle and/or say the correct answer.

1. What is a fruit when it is ready to eat?

wipe　　　**ripe**

2. What do you do to a plate when it is wet?

wipe　　　**ripe**

3. What large mammal swims in the ocean?

whale　　　**rail**

4. What do you hold onto as you walk up stairs?

whale　　　**rail**

5. What do you use to cook?

wok　　　**rock**

6. What do you find outside on the ground?

wok　　　**rock**

7. What do you use to clean?

wag　　　**rag**

8. What does a dog do with his tail?

wag　　　**rag**

9. What do you NOT want to grow in the garden?

weed　　　**read**

10. What do you do to a book?

weed　　　**read**

_____ _____ _____
　　　　　Name　　　　　　　　　　Date　　　　　　　Homework Partner

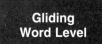

Gliding Word Level

Minimal Contrast Definitions

Directions: Read each question and possible answers aloud. Ask students to circle and/or say the correct answer.

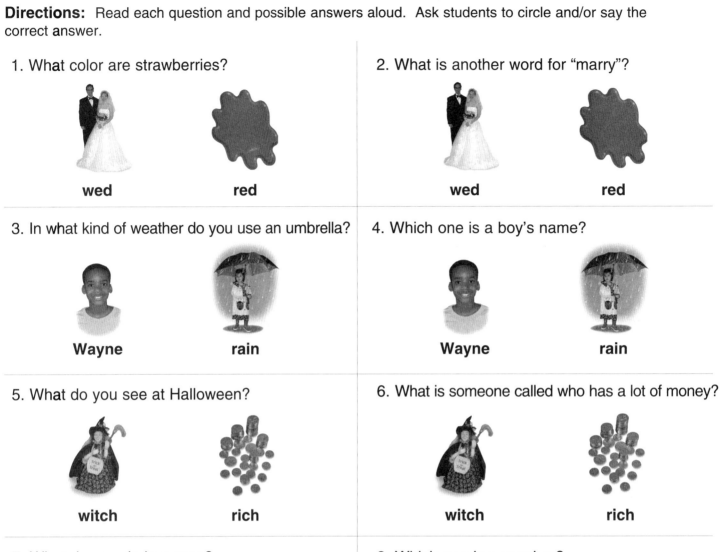

1. What color are strawberries?

wed   **red**

2. What is another word for "marry"?

wed   **red**

3. In what kind of weather do you use an umbrella?

Wayne   **rain**

4. Which one is a boy's name?

Wayne   **rain**

5. What do you see at Halloween?

witch   **rich**

6. What is someone called who has a lot of money?

witch   **rich**

7. What do you do in a race?

one   **run**

8. Which one is a number?

one   **run**

9. What do you do when you take a nap?

west   **rest**

10. Which one is a direction?

west   **rest**

_____ _____ _____

Name   Date   Homework Partner

Gliding Word Level

#BK-320 Webber® Photo Phonology Minimal Pair Cards Fun Sheets • ©2005 Super Duper® Publications • www.superduperinc.com • 1-800-277-8737

Minimal Contrast Definitions

Directions: Read each question and possible answers aloud. Ask students to circle and/or say the correct answer.

1. What does a bird use to fly?

wing **ring**

2. What jewelry do you wear on your fing**er**?

wing **ring**

3. Which one is part of a fishing rod?

wheel **reel**

4. Which one is part of a wagon?

wheel **reel**

5. What do you do with a pencil?

white **write**

6. Which one is a color?

white **write**

7. Seven days makes a...

week **leak**

8. What does a dripping faucet do?

week **leak**

9. What do you do to an ice cream cone?

wick **lick**

10. What is part of a candle?

wick **lick**

Gliding Word Level

_____ _____ _____
Name Date Homework Partner

Minimal Contrast Definitions

Directions: Read each question and possible answers aloud. Ask students to circle and/or say the correct answer.

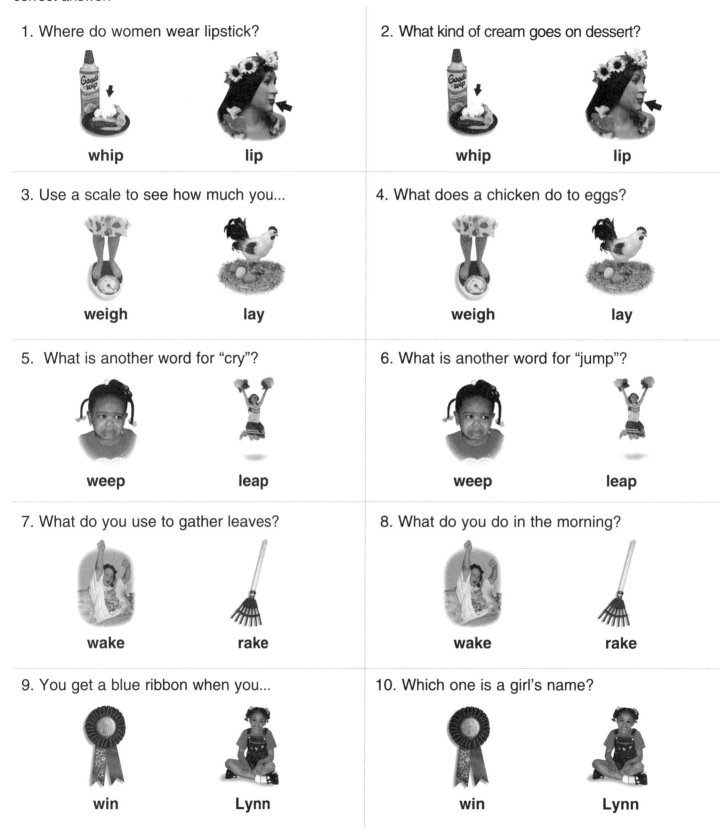

1. Where do women wear lipstick?

   whip   **lip**

2. What kind of cream goes on dessert?

   whip   **lip**

3. Use a scale to see how much you...

   weigh   **lay**

4. What does a chicken do to eggs?

   weigh   **lay**

5. What is another word for "cry"?

   weep   **leap**

6. What is another word for "jump"?

   weep   **leap**

7. What do you use to gather leaves?

   wake   **rake**

8. What do you do in the morning?

   wake   **rake**

9. You get a blue ribbon when you...

   win   **Lynn**

10. Which one is a girl's name?

    win   **Lynn**

_____ _____ _____

Name   Date   Homework Partner

Gliding Word Level

#BK-320 Webber® Photo Phonology Minimal Pair Cards Fun Sheets • ©2005 Super Duper® Publications • www.superduperinc.com • 1-800-277-8737

Minimal Contrast Definitions

Directions: Read each question and possible answers aloud. Ask students to circle and/or say the correct answer.

1. Who knows many magic spells and potions?

wizard   **lizard**

2. Which one is a reptile?

wizard   **lizard**

3. What does a four-leaf clover represent?

yuck   **luck**

4. What does a kid say when he doesn't like a vegetable?

yuck   **luck**

5. What is a baby sheep called?

yam   **lamb**

6. Which one is a vegetable?

yam   **lamb**

7. Use a mower to cut the...

yawn   **lawn**

8. What do you do when you are sleepy?

yawn   **lawn**

9. What does a duck say?

quack   **crack**

10. What do you do to an egg?

quack   **crack**

_____ _____ _____

Name   Date   Homework Partner

Gliding Word Level

Minimal Contrast Definitions

Directions: Read each question and possible answers aloud. Ask students to circle and/or say the correct answer.

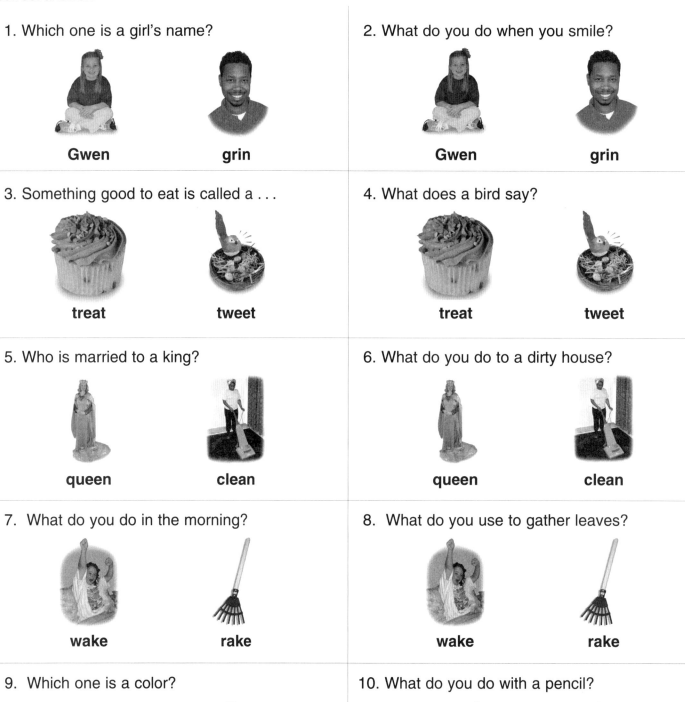

1. Which one is a girl's name?

   Gwen   **grin**

2. What do you do when you smile?

   Gwen   **grin**

3. Something good to eat is called a . . .

   treat   **tweet**

4. What does a bird say?

   treat   **tweet**

5. Who is married to a king?

   queen   **clean**

6. What do you do to a dirty house?

   queen   **clean**

7. What do you do in the morning?

   wake   **rake**

8. What do you use to gather leaves?

   wake   **rake**

9. Which one is a color?

   white   **write**

10. What do you do with a pencil?

    white   **write**

Name   Date   Homework Partner

Gliding Word Level

#BK-320 Webber® Photo Phonology Minimal Pair Cards Fun Sheets • ©2005 Super Duper® Publications • www.superduperinc.com • 1-800-277-8737

Pick a Tulip

Directions: Cut out the tulips below. Glue, tape, or place each tulip onto a stem as you read/say each picture-word aloud.

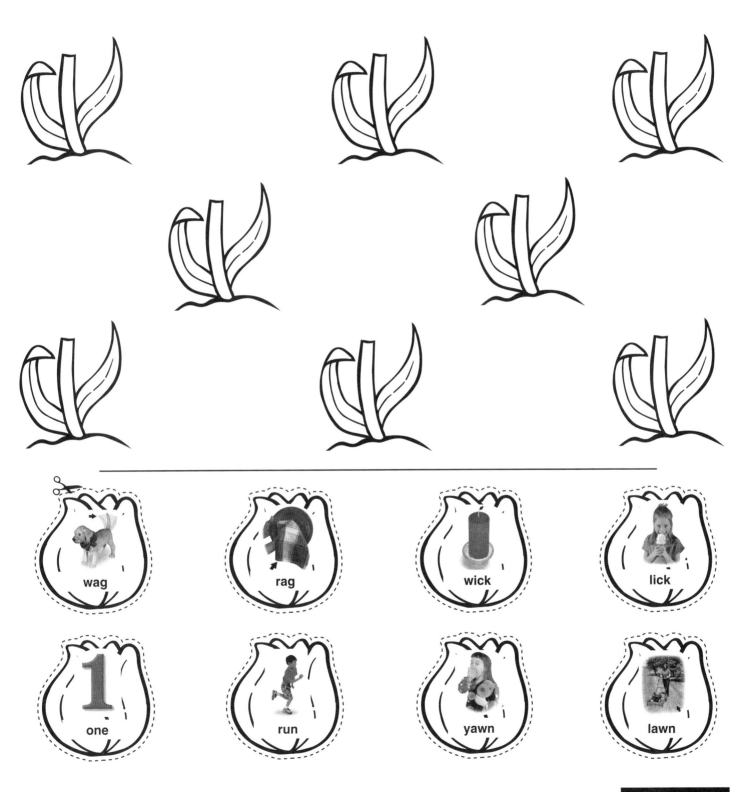

wag

rag

wick

lick

one

run

yawn

lawn

_____   _____   _____

Name   Date   Homework Partner

Sound Sorter

Directions: Read/say each picture-word aloud. Listen to the first sound in each word. Cross out the picture and/or pictures that do not start with the R sound.

ripe

wipe

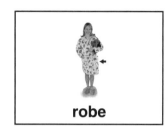
robe

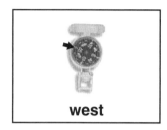
west

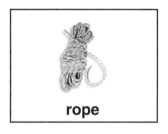
rope

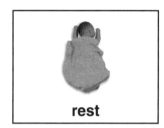
rest

rock

wing

wok

rain

Wayne

rice

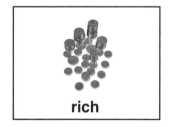
rich

wig

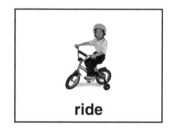
ride

witch

rail

whale

race

raise

Name   Date   Homework Partner

Gliding Word Level

#BK-320 Webber® Photo Phonology Minimal Pair Cards Fun Sheets • ©2005 Super Duper® Publications • www.superduperinc.com • 1-800-277-8737

Balloon Bounce

Directions: Read/say aloud the picture-words below. Then, cut out the markers. Flip a coin (heads=1, tails=2) to determine how many spaces to move. As you move, read/say each picture-word aloud. First player to reach the finish wins.

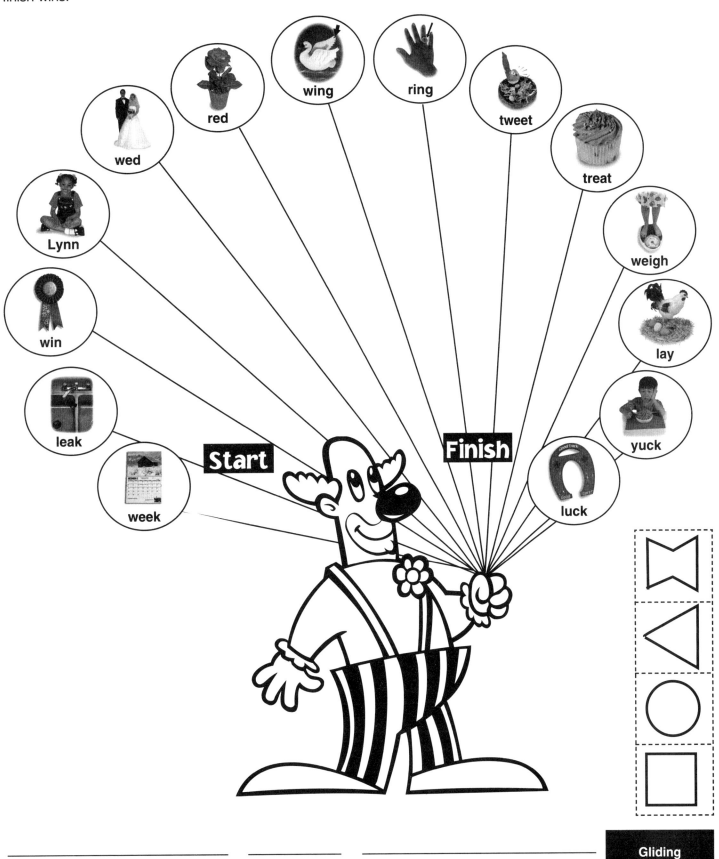

Sweet Treat

Directions: Cut out the candy below and place them face down in a pile. As you choose a piece of candy, read/say aloud the picture-word on it and glue, tape, or place the candy onto the candy jar.

wheel	reel	whip	lip	weep	leap	wizard
yam	lamb	Gwen	grin	queen	clean	lizard

Name   Date   Homework Partner

#BK-320 Webber® Photo Phonology Minimal Pair Cards Fun Sheets • ©2005 Super Duper® Publications • www.superduperinc.com • 1-800-277-8737

Phrase Racing

Directions: Cut out a car for each player and put at the starting line. Flip a coin to determine how many spaces to move (heads=2, tails=1). Read/say aloud each phrase as you land on it. First one to the Finish wins!

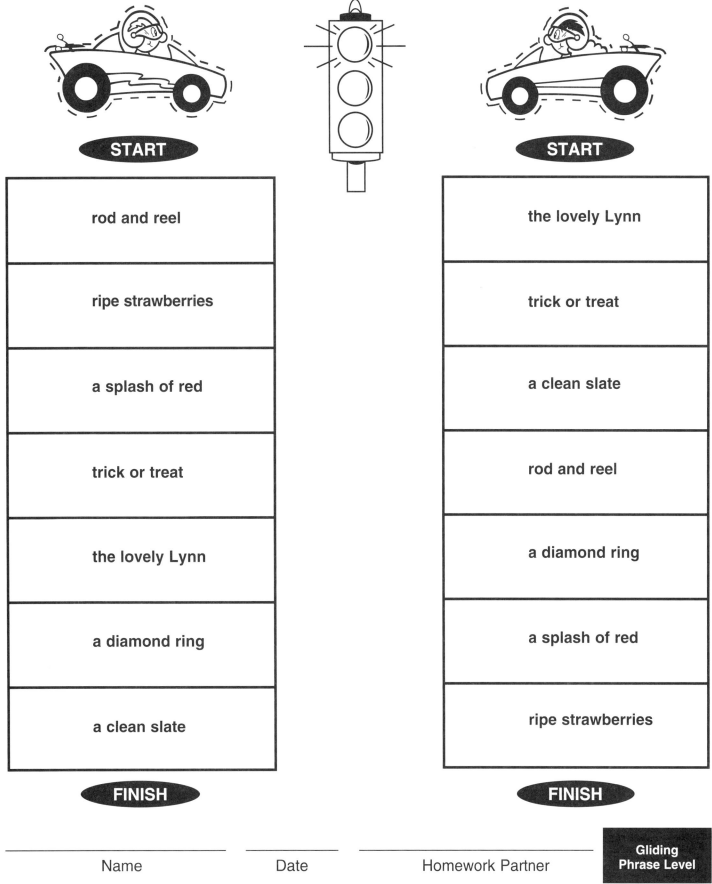

START	START
rod and reel	the lovely Lynn
ripe strawberries	trick or treat
a splash of red	a clean slate
trick or treat	rod and reel
the lovely Lynn	a diamond ring
a diamond ring	a splash of red
a clean slate	ripe strawberries
FINISH	FINISH

_____ _____ _____

Name   Date   Homework Partner

Gliding Phrase Level

Go-Together Match-Ups

Directions: Draw a line from the word in Column A to the word that goes with it in Column B. Read/say each phrase aloud *("read book")*.

A		B
read		mower
lawn		storm
write		ice cream
rain		leaves
rake		book
lick		race
run		letter

_____ _____ _____

Name   Date   Homework Partner

Gliding Phrase Level

#BK-320 Webber® Photo Phonology Minimal Pair Cards Fun Sheets • ©2005 Super Duper® Publications • www.superduperinc.com • 1-800-277-8737

Fold Again

Directions: Fold this page along the dotted lines so that the arrows at the top meet. Read/say aloud the phrases you see using the describing word and the picture-word *("**lick** ice cream")*.

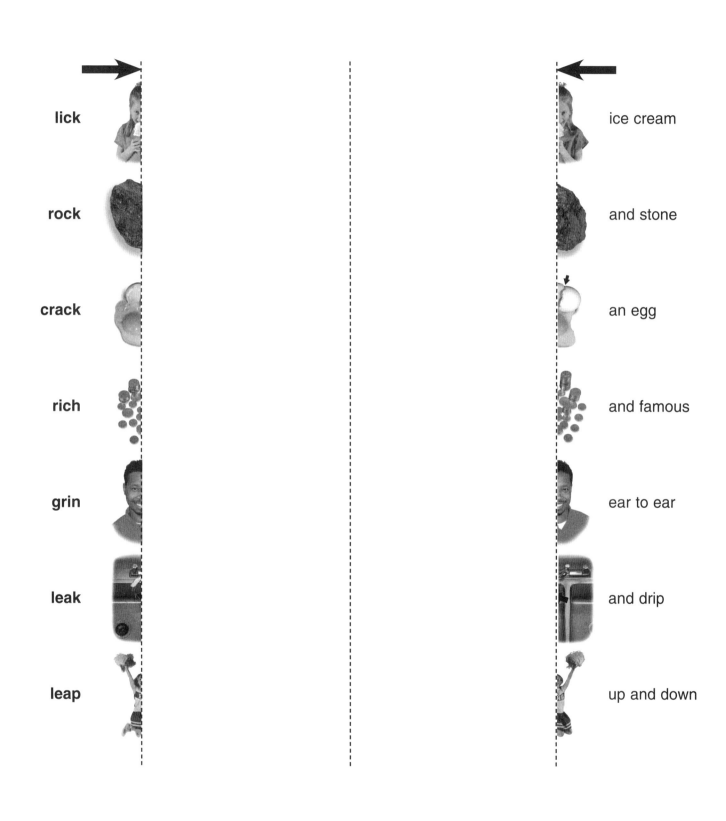

lick	ice cream
rock	and stone
crack	an egg
rich	and famous
grin	ear to ear
leak	and drip
leap	up and down

Name   Date   Homework Partner

Mine or Yours?

Directions: Read/say each picture-word below. Cut out the pictures and put face down in a pile. Turn over a picture and flip a coin. Heads means you keep the picture and say, *"my _____"* (*"my <u>whale</u>"*). Tails means you give the picture to your partner and say, *"your _____"* (*"your <u>whale</u>"*). Most pictures at the end wins.

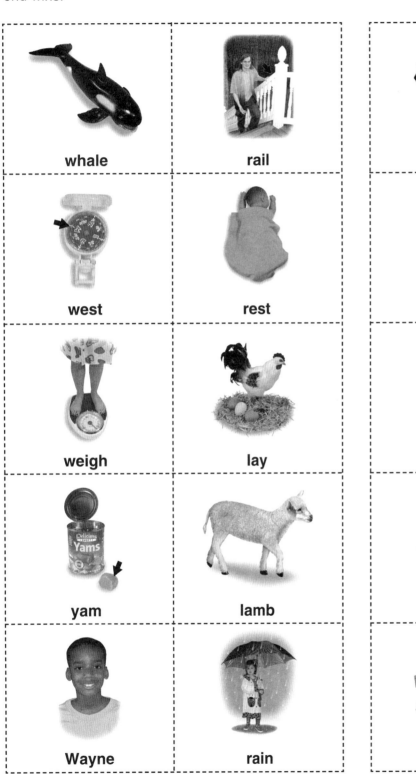

whale	rail
west	rest
weigh	lay
yam	lamb
Wayne	rain

wag	rag
whip	lip
wizard	lizard
wake	rake
wheel	reel

_____ _____ _____

Name　　　　　　　　Date　　　　　Homework Partner

#BK-320 Webber® Photo Phonology Minimal Pair Cards Fun Sheets • ©2005 Super Duper® Publications • www.superduperinc.com • 1-800-277-8737

"I would..."

Directions: Read/say the questions below. Answer them aloud, using the target word in a sentence. *("I would like a **ripe** apple.")*

1. If you could have fruit, what would you like?

   ripe

2. If you could have any , what would you choose?

   treat

3. If you had good , what would you wish?

   luck

4. If you were , what would you buy?

   rich

5. If you found a magic , what would it do?

   rock

6. If you could as high as the sky, what would you see?

   leap

7. If you found a diamond , what would you do with it?

   ring

_____   _____   _____   **Gliding Sentence Level**
Name   Date   Homework Partner

Replace It

Directions: Read/say each sentence below. Change the underlined word in the sentence so that it makes sense using a picture-word from the Word Bank. Then, read/say the corrected sentence aloud.

Word Bank

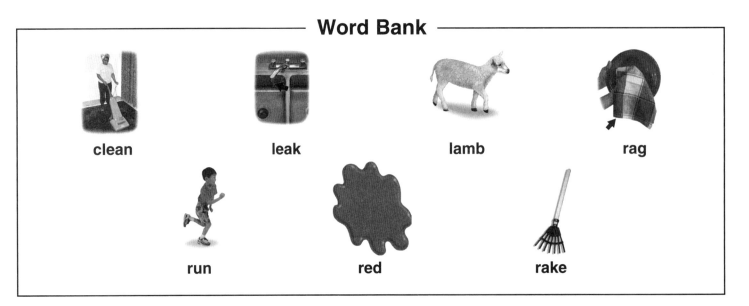

clean   leak   lamb   rag

run   red   rake

1. Dry the dishes with a <u>shoe</u>.

2. <u>Skip</u> in a race.

3. A <u>bird</u> says "baa baa."

4. The kitchen faucet may <u>scream</u>.

5. <u>Pineapple</u> is a color.

6. A <u>diaper</u> is a tool.

7. Use a vacuum to <u>cook</u>.

Answer Key: 1. rag 2. run 3. lamb 4. leak 5. red 6. rake 7. clean

Name _____ Date _____ Homework Partner _____

Gliding Sentence Level

#BK-320 Webber® Photo Phonology Minimal Pair Cards Fun Sheets • ©2005 Super Duper® Publications • www.superduperinc.com • 1-800-277-8737

One, Two, Three

Directions: Each student gets three turns to roll the die. The number on the die corresponds to the number next to the phrase to be used in a silly sentence. For example, a student who rolls a two, five, and one will make a sentence with the phrases: *"The farm animal likes to rest for the principal."*

	Roll One	Roll Two	Roll Three
	1. The teacher	will read	for the principal.
	2. The farm animal	likes to lick Kool-aid	off the farmer's hands.
	3. The little boy	played the piano	on the lawn.
	4. My friend Lynn	eats popcorn	for breakfast.
	5. The silly puppy	likes to rest	on the counter.
	6. The weatherman	said it may rain	at the picnic.

_____ _____ _____

Name   Date   Homework Partner

Gliding Sentence Level

Spin a Sentence

Directions: Read/say aloud the picture-words below. If you prefer, glue this page to construction paper for added durability. Cut out the arrow/dial. Use a brad to connect the dial to the circle. Spin the spinner. When you land on a sentence, complete the sentence by choosing the correct picture. Read/say the sentence aloud.

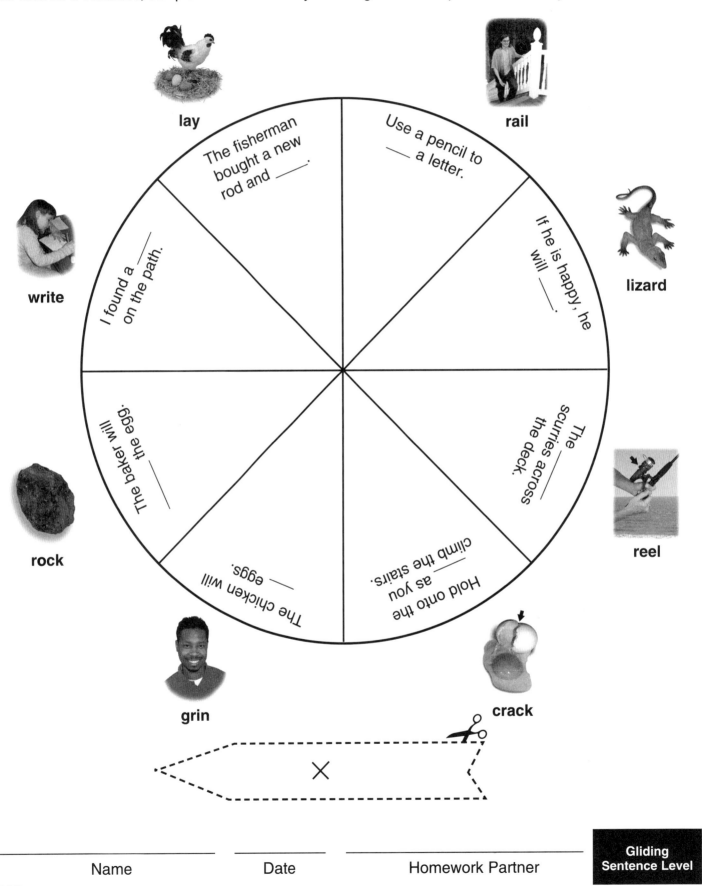

lay

rail

write

lizard

rock

reel

grin

crack

The fisherman bought a new rod and ___.

Use a pencil to ___ a letter.

If he is happy, he will ___.

I found a ___ on the path.

The ___ scurries across the deck.

The baker will ___ the egg.

Hold onto the ___ as you climb the stairs.

The chicken will ___ eggs.

Gliding Sentence Level

Auditory Bombardment

Directions: Have the student listen carefully as you read the following list of words slowly and clearly. The student does not need to repeat the words, but just listen to them. You may have the student engage in a quiet activity, like coloring, as you read.

1. park	34. tub	67. feast
2. pie	35. tool	68. find
3. peach	36. top	69. fold
4. pat	37. tongue	70. fetch
5. pass	38. taste	71. fern
6. puck	39. tea	72. four
7. push	40. tax	73. fair
8. path	41. cold	74. fast
9. pole	42. coat	75. feed
10. pear	43. coast	76. fat
11. peas	44. curl	77. fence
12. pack	45. card	78. field
13. page	46. Kate	79. fight
14. pearl	47. cat	80. fig
15. pile	48. comb	81. sip
16. point	49. corn	82. Sue
17. purse	50. cash	83. son
18. patch	51. carve	84. sand
19. pen	52. cut	85. sing
20. pipe	53. key	86. sour
21. tip	54. king	87. sock
22. town	55. kiss	88. sail
23. tot	56. kite	89. soup
24. time	57. court	90. seed
25. toe	58. cone	91. sat
26. test	59. cow	92. soap
27. tail	60. catch	93. sack
28. tan	61. fan	94. sink
29. team	62. face	95. safe
30. toad	63. fun	96. sigh
31. toast	64. farm	97. salt
32. turn	65. fur	98. sub
33. toy	66. fork	99. surf
		100. sign

Name _____ Date _____ Homework Partner _____

Prevocalic Voicing Word Level

Minimal Contrast Pairs

Directions: Have student point to picture-words as teacher/helper says each word aloud.

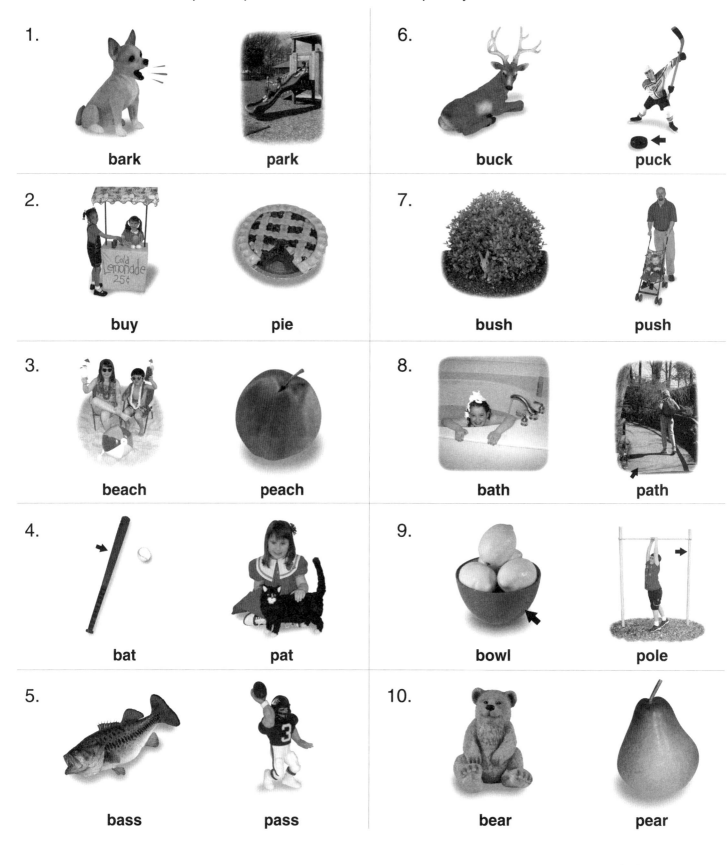

1. bark   park

2. buy   pie

3. beach   peach

4. bat   pat

5. bass   pass

6. buck   puck

7. bush   push

8. bath   path

9. bowl   pole

10. bear   pear

_____ _____ _____

Name   Date   Homework Partner

Prevocalic Voicing Word Level

#BK-320 Webber® Photo Phonology Minimal Pair Cards Fun Sheets • ©2005 Super Duper® Publications • 1-800-277-8737 • Online! www.superduperinc.com

Minimal Contrast Pairs

Directions: Have student point to picture-words as teacher/helper says each word aloud.

1. dip   tip

2. down   town

3. dot   tot

4. dime   time

5. dough   toe

6. deer   tear

7. gold   cold

8. goat   coat

9. ghost   coast

10. gate   Kate

_____ _____ _____

Name   Date   Homework Partner

Prevocalic Voicing Word Level

Minimal Contrast Pairs

Directions: Have student point to picture-words as teacher/helper says each word aloud.

1.

girl   curl

2.

guard   card

3.

gate   Kate

4.

van   fan

5.

vase   face

6.

zip   sip

7.

zoo   Sue

8.

bark   park

9.

bees   peas

10.

back   pack

_____   _____   _____

Name   Date   Homework Partner

Prevocalic Voicing Word Level

#BK-320 Webber® Photo Phonology Minimal Pair Cards Fun Sheets • ©2005 Super Duper® Publications • 1-800-277-8737 • Online! www.superduperinc.com

Minimal Contrast Definitions

Directions: Read each question and possible answers aloud. Ask students to circle and/or say the correct answer.

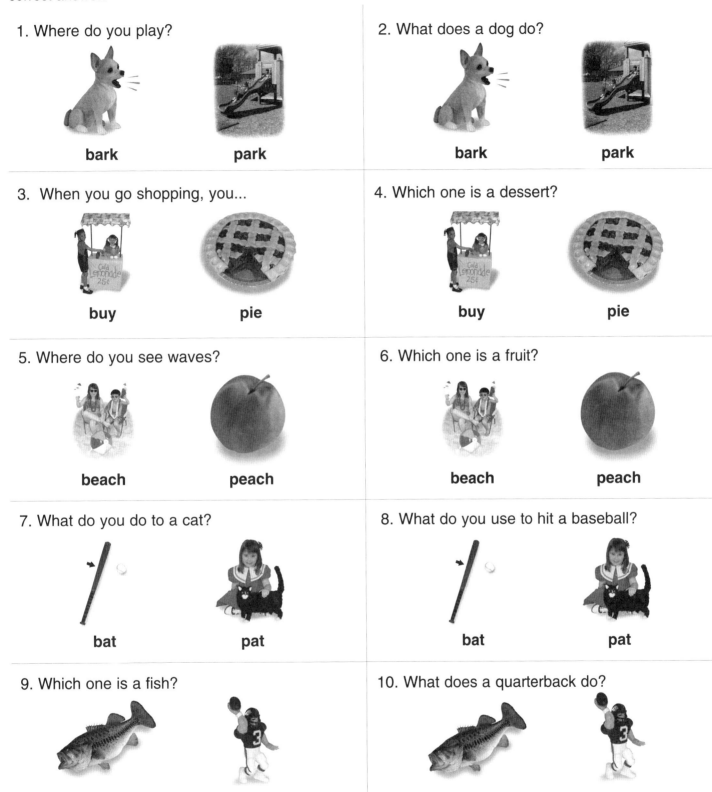

1. Where do you play?

    bark   **park**

2. What does a dog do?

    bark   **park**

3. When you go shopping, you...

    buy   **pie**

4. Which one is a dessert?

    buy   **pie**

5. Where do you see waves?

    beach   **peach**

6. Which one is a fruit?

    beach   **peach**

7. What do you do to a cat?

    bat   **pat**

8. What do you use to hit a baseball?

    bat   **pat**

9. Which one is a fish?

    bass   **pass**

10. What does a quarterback do?

    bass   **pass**

_____ _____ _____
Name   Date   Homework Partner

Minimal Contrast Definitions

Directions: Read each question and possible answers aloud. Ask students to circle and/or say the correct answer.

1. What does a hockey player hit?

   buck   **puck**

2. Which one is a male deer?

   buck   **puck**

3. What grows in the yard?

   bush   **push**

4. What do you do to a stroller?

   bush   **push**

5. In the tub, you take a . . .

   bath   **path**

6. Where do you walk in the park?

   bath   **path**

7. What holds food?

   bowl   **pole**

8. What can you climb?

   bowl   **pole**

9. Which one is a fruit?

   bear   **pear**

10. Which one is an animal?

   bear   **pear**

_____   _____   _____
          Name   Date   Homework Partner

Prevocalic Voicing Word Level

#BK-320 Webber® Photo Phonology Minimal Pair Cards Fun Sheets • ©2005 Super Duper® Publications • 1-800-277-8737 • Online! www.superduperinc.com

Minimal Contrast Definitions

Directions: Read each question and possible answers aloud. Ask students to circle and/or say the correct answer.

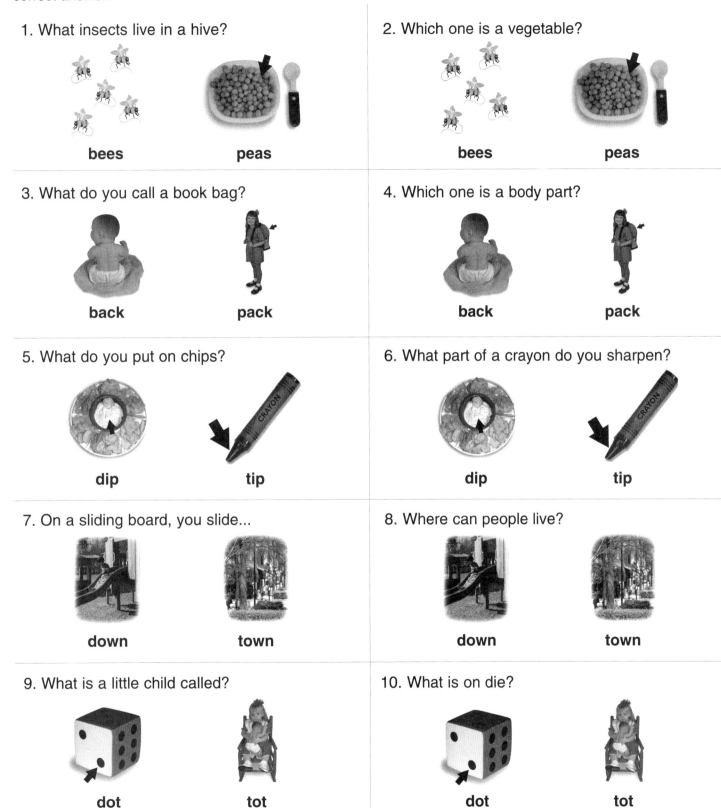

1. What insects live in a hive?

   bees   **peas**

2. Which one is a vegetable?

   bees   **peas**

3. What do you call a book bag?

   back   **pack**

4. Which one is a body part?

   back   **pack**

5. What do you put on chips?

   dip   **tip**

6. What part of a crayon do you sharpen?

   dip   **tip**

7. On a sliding board, you slide...

   down   **town**

8. Where can people live?

   down   **town**

9. What is a little child called?

   dot   **tot**

10. What is on die?

    dot   **tot**

_____   _____   _____

Name   Date   Homework Partner

Minimal Contrast Definitions

Directions: Read each question and possible answers aloud. Ask students to circle and/or say the correct answer.

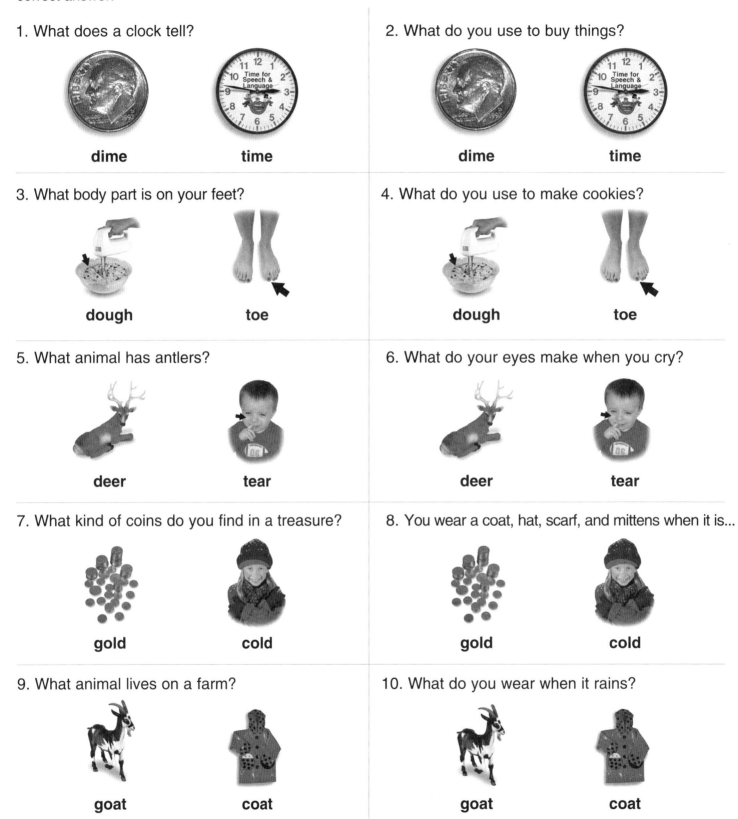

1. What does a clock tell?

dime   time

2. What do you use to buy things?

dime   time

3. What body part is on your feet?

dough   toe

4. What do you use to make cookies?

dough   toe

5. What animal has antlers?

deer   tear

6. What do your eyes make when you cry?

deer   tear

7. What kind of coins do you find in a treasure?

gold   cold

8. You wear a coat, hat, scarf, and mittens when it is...

gold   cold

9. What animal lives on a farm?

goat   coat

10. What do you wear when it rains?

goat   coat

_____   _____   _____
Name   Date   Homework Partner

Prevocalic Voicing Word Level

#BK-320 Webber® Photo Phonology Minimal Pair Cards Fun Sheets • ©2005 Super Duper® Publications • 1-800-277-8737 • Online! www.superduperinc.com

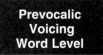

Minimal Contrast Definitions

Directions: Read each question and possible answers aloud. Ask students to circle and/or say the correct answer.

1. What is another name for the beach?

ghost   **coast**

2. What do you see at Halloween?

ghost   **coast**

3. Who wears a dress?

girl   **curl**

4. What can your hair do?

girl   **curl**

5. Who helps you cross the street?

guard   **card**

6. What do you need to play "Go Fish"?

guard   **card**

7. Which one is a girl's name?

gate   **Kate**

8. What part of the fence opens and closes?

gate   **Kate**

9. Which one is a vehicle?

van   **fan**

10. Which one blows air?

van   **fan**

_____ _____ _____

Name   Date   Homework Partner

Prevocalic Voicing Word Level

Minimal Contrast Definitions

Directions: Read each question and possible answers aloud. Ask student to circle and/or say the correct answer.

1. Which one is a body part?

    vase   face

2. What do you use for holding flowers?

    vase   face

3. What do you do with a zipper?

    zip   sip

4. What do you do at the water fountain?

    zip   sip

5. Which one is a girl's name?

    zoo   Sue

6. Where do you see many different animals?

    zoo   Sue

7. What part of a crayon do you sharpen?

    dip   tip

8. What do you put on chips?

    dip   tip

9. Where do you walk in the park?

    bath   path

10. In the tub, you take a . . .

    bath   path

_____ _____ _____

Name   Date   Homework Partner

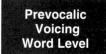

Prevocalic Voicing Word Level

#BK-320 Webber® Photo Phonology Minimal Pair Cards Fun Sheets • ©2005 Super Duper® Publications • 1-800-277-8737 • Online! www.superduperinc.com

Ice Cream Scoops

Directions: Read/say aloud the picture-words below. Then, cut out the ice cream cones and scoop cards. Each player gets a cone. The first player reads/says the picture-word on a scoop card and places it on his/her cone. Play continues in turn.

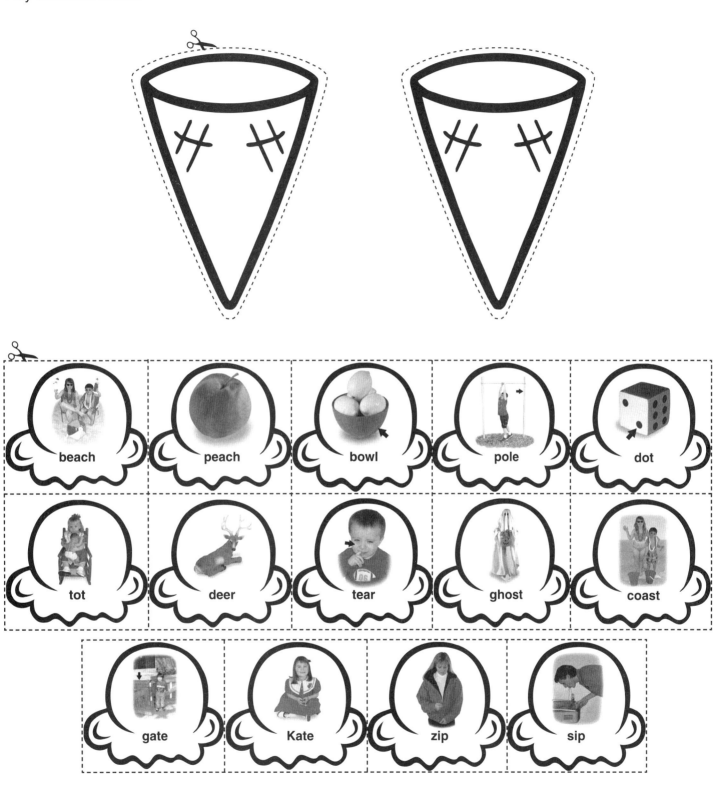

beach	peach	bowl	pole	dot
tot	deer	tear	ghost	coast
gate	Kate	zip	sip	

_____ _____ _____
Name   Date   Homework Partner

Sound Sorter

Directions: Read/say each picture-word aloud. Listen to the first sound in each word. Cross out the picture and/or pictures that do not start with the P sound. Then, read/say aloud only the words that begin with the P sound.

pear

bear

pug

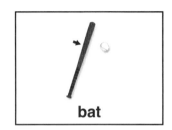
bat

pat

pig

path

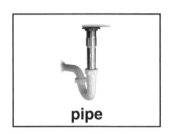
pipe

bath

buy

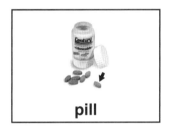
pill

pants

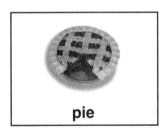
pie

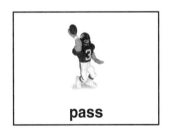
pass

bass

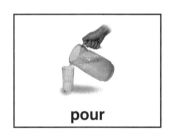
pour

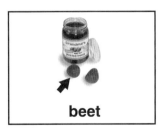
beet

peas

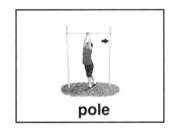
pole

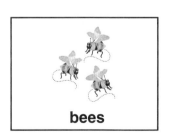
bees

Name   Date   Homework Partner

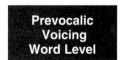
Prevocalic Voicing Word Level

#BK-320 Webber® Photo Phonology Minimal Pair Cards Fun Sheets • ©2005 Super Duper® Publications • 1-800-277-8737 • Online! www.superduperinc.com

Floating Clouds

Directions: Read/say aloud the picture-words below. Then, cut out the markers. Begin at start and flip a coin (heads=1, tails=2) to determine how many spaces to move. As you move, read/say each picture-word aloud. First player to reach the finish wins.

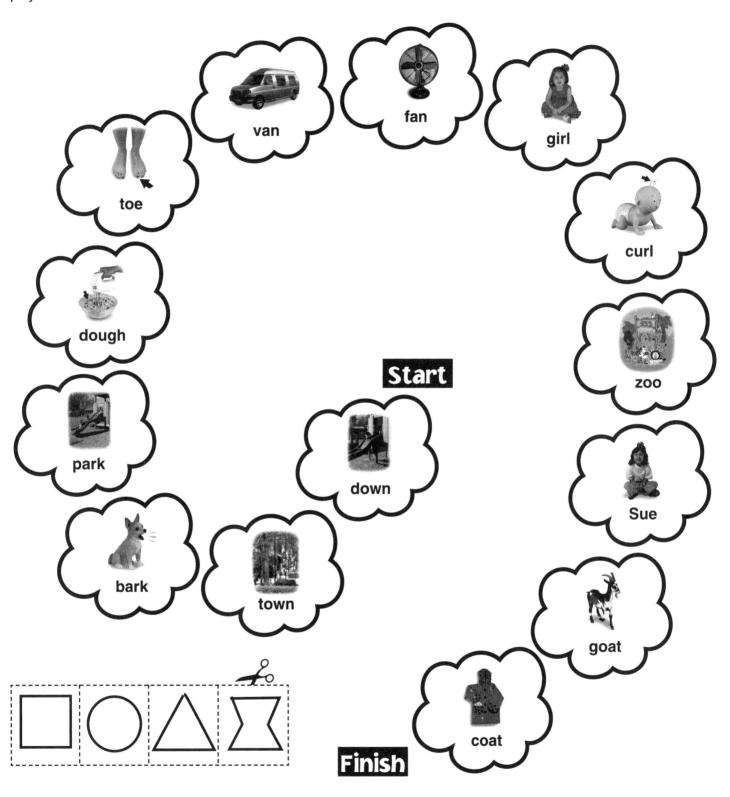

Slide and Say

Directions: Read/say aloud the picture-words below. Then, cut out all the cards. "Slide" the cards down the slide, reading/saying each word aloud as you slide.

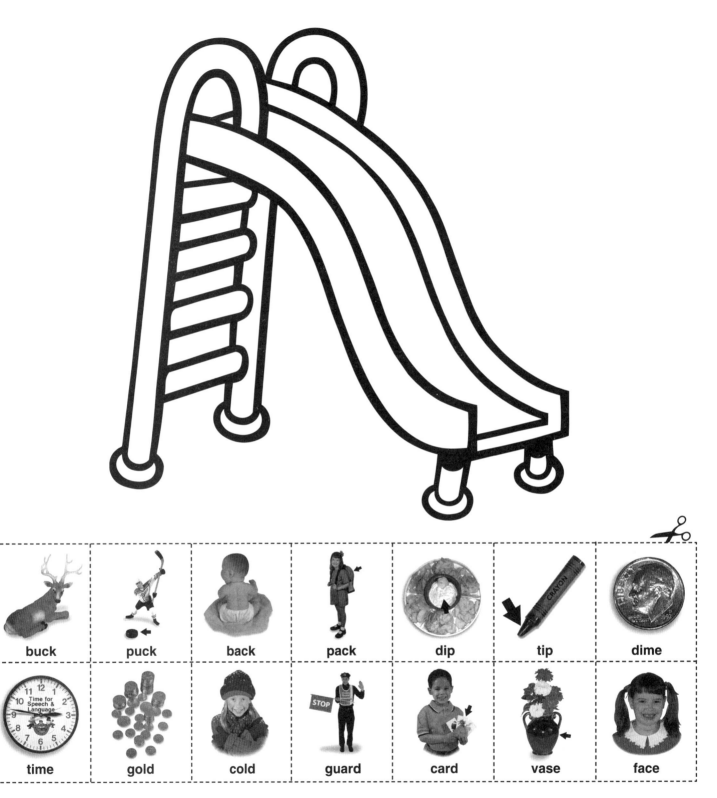

buck	puck	back	pack	dip	tip	dime
time	gold	cold	guard	card	vase	face

Name   Date   Homework Partner

Prevocalic Voicing Word Level

Answer It!

Directions: Read each question below and choose the phrase that best answers it. Put an X beside the correct answer. Read/say the phrases aloud.

1. What do you wear?

_____ a) a toy car

_____ b) a big coat

2. What do you eat?

_____ a) yummy peas

_____ b) a pine tree

3. What can you eat with ice cream?

_____ a) cherry pie

_____ b) a bat and ball

4. Which one is sports equipment?

_____ a) a math book

_____ b) a black puck

5. Which fruit is fuzzy?

_____ a) a ripe peach

_____ b) a juicy orange

6. What makes you cool when it's hot outside?

_____ a) a refrigerator

_____ b) a new fan

7. What can you wiggle?

_____ a) my house

_____ b) my big toe

Answer Key: 1.b 2.a 3.a 4.b 5.a 6.b 7.b

_____   _____   _____

Name   Date   Homework Partner

Prevocalic Voicing Phrase Level

Phrase Fill-In

Directions: Write a vowel in each blank space below to spell the words correctly. Then read/say each phrase aloud.

1. p__t s___ftly

2. a b__g t__ar

3. a h__ppy fac__

4. a p__ar tre__

5. p__sh and p__ll

6. a l__ttle t__wn

Answer Key: 1. a, o 2. i, e 3. a, e 4. e, e 5. u, u 6. i, o

#BK-320 Webber® Photo Phonology Minimal Pair Cards Fun Sheets • ©2005 Super Duper® Publications • 1-800-277-8737 • Online! www.superduperinc.com

_____ _____ _____

Name   Date   Homework Partner

Prevocalic Voicing Phrase Level

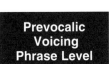

Puzzle Match

Directions: Draw a line from a puzzle piece in Column A to the one that matches it in Column B. Read/say the completed phrase aloud.

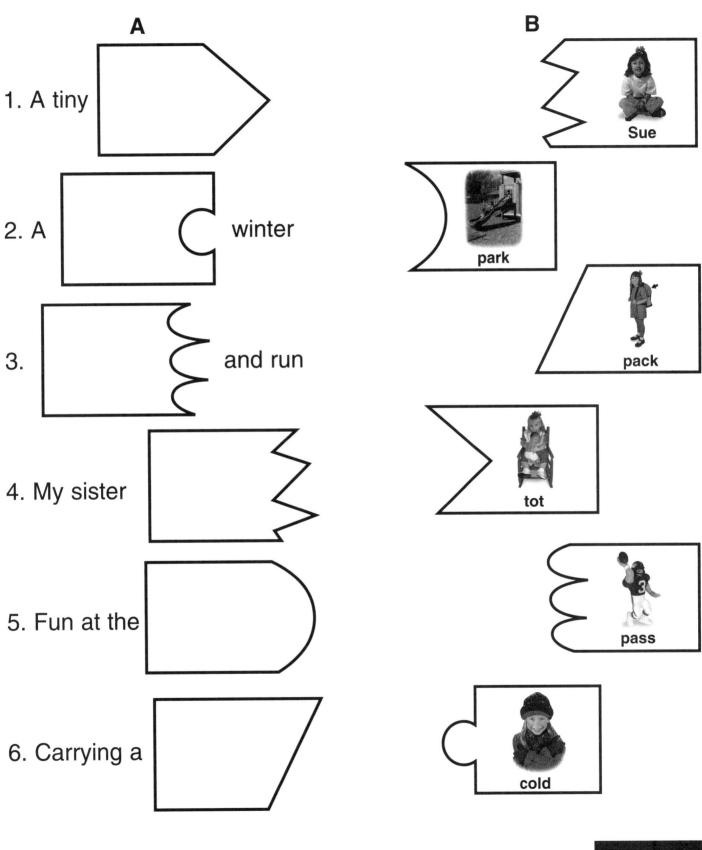

A

1. A tiny

2. A   winter

3.   and run

4. My sister

5. Fun at the

6. Carrying a

B

Sue

park

pack

tot

pass

cold

Name   Date   Homework Partner

Fix It! Phrases

Directions: Each phrase below has an underlined incorrect letter in it. Fix each phrase by saying/circling the correct letter on the right side of the book. Read/say aloud each correct phrase.

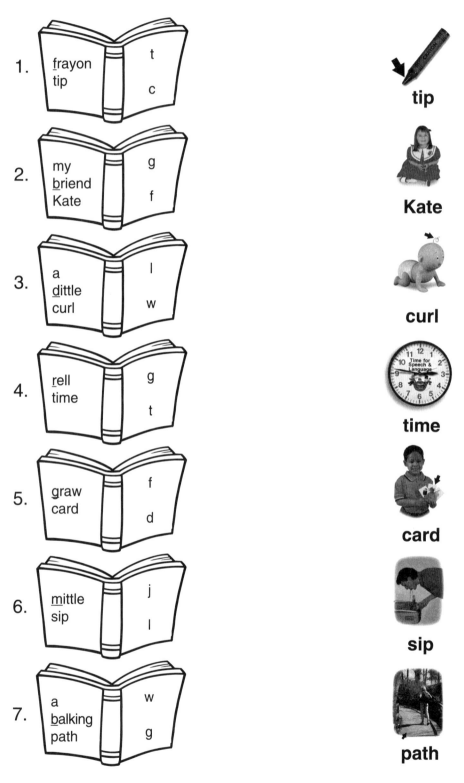

1. <u>f</u>rayon tip — t / c

tip

2. my <u>b</u>riend Kate — g / f

Kate

3. a <u>d</u>ittle curl — l / w

curl

4. <u>r</u>ell time — g / t

time

5. <u>g</u>raw card — f / d

card

6. <u>m</u>ittle sip — j / l

sip

7. a <u>b</u>alking path — w / g

path

Answer Key: 1. c 2. f 3. l 4. t 5. d 6. l 7. w

_____   _____   _____

Name   Date   Homework Partner

Prevocalic Voicing Phrase Level

#BK-320 Webber® Photo Phonology Minimal Pair Cards Fun Sheets • ©2005 Super Duper® Publications • 1-800-277-8737 • Online! www.superduperinc.com

Sentence Fill-In

Directions: Draw a line from the sentence in Column A to the picture-word that completes it in Column B.

A

1. The _____ played with toys.

2. Turn on the _____.

3. They live on the _____.

4. Mom said to eat your _____.

5. I like to play at the _____.

6. Wear your coat when it's _____.

7. The goalie stopped the _____.

B

coast

cold

park

puck

tot

fan

peas

Which One?

Directions: Read/say each picture-word on the right. Then, answer each question by circling the correct answer. Read/say each answer aloud using a complete sentence.

1. Which one keeps you warm?

    coat   dime

2. Which one wiggles?

    zoo   toe

3. Which one do you bake?

    gold   pie

4. Which one do you wear?

    pack   bat

5. Which one do you climb?

    zip   pole

6. Which one do you eat?

    pear   van

7. Which one is a person?

    Kate   bear

Answer Key: 1. coat 2. toe 3. pie 4. pack 5. pole 6. pear 7. Kate

Name   Date   Homework Partner

#BK-320 Webber® Photo Phonology Minimal Pair Cards Fun Sheets • ©2005 Super Duper® Publications • 1-800-277-8737 • Online! www.superduperinc.com

Coat Closet

Directions: Read/say aloud the picture-words on each shirt. Cut out the dollar bills below. Give a dollar bill to your teacher/homework partner as you pick out something to buy. Say,*"I want to buy a _____."*

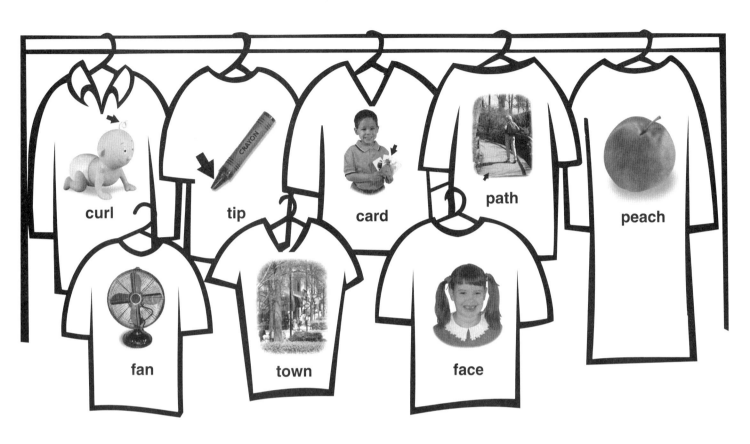

curl

tip

card

path

peach

fan

town

face

_____ _____ _____

Name   Date   Homework Partner

Scrambled Sentences

Directions: Unscramble each sentence and write it on the line below the egg. Then, read/say the sentence aloud.

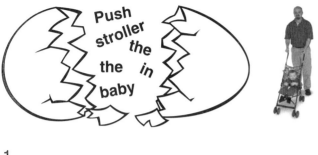

1. _____

_____ .

2. _____

_____ .

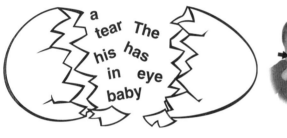

3. _____

_____ .

4. _____

_____ .

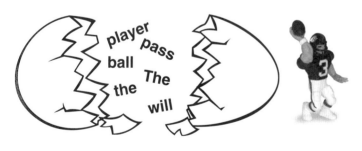

5. _____

_____ .

6. _____

_____ .

_____ _____ _____

Name   Date   Homework Partner

Prevocalic Voicing Sentence Level

#BK-320 Webber® Photo Phonology Minimal Pair Cards Fun Sheets • ©2005 Super Duper® Publications • 1-800-277-8737 • Online! www.superduperinc.com

Auditory Bombardment

Directions: Have the student listen carefully as you read the following list of words slowly and clearly. The student does not need to repeat the words, but just listen to them. You may have the student engage in a quiet activity, like coloring, as you read.

1. bug	34. bed	67. tease
2. tag	35. thread	68. squeeze
3. rag	36. blade	69. sneeze
4. pug	37. cloud	70. robe
5. pig	38. bread	71. cob
6. log	39. dad	72. cub
7. bag	40. maid	73. lab
8. dug	41. shed	74. rib
9. wig	42. tide	75. club
10. big	43. dude	76. cube
11. dog	44. feed	77. crib
12. egg	45. good	78. globe
13. fig	46. lad	79. knob
14. flag	47. kid	80. web
15. frog	48. hide	81. tub
16. hog	49. road	82. crab
17. twig	50. food	83. cab
18. slug	51. buzz	84. job
19. jog	52. eyes	85. save
20. plug	53. fuzz	86. leave
21. jug	54. knees	87. hive
22. mug	55. raise	88. pave
23. leg	56. rise	89. love
24. brag	57. peas	90. five
25. mad	58. cheese	91. give
26. ride	59. prize	92. cave
27. sad	60. freeze	93. glove
28. seed	61. fries	94. brave
29. lid	62. graze	95. sleeve
30. add	63. hose	96. wave
31. bead	64. jazz	97. dive
32. wood	65. noise	98. dove
33. toad	66. maze	99. grove
		100. stove

_____   _____   _____

Name   Date   Homework Partner

Postvocalic Devoicing Word Level

Minimal Contrast Pairs

Directions: Have student point to picture-words as teacher/helper says each word aloud.

1.
buck   **bug**

6.
lock   **log**

2.
tack   **tag**

7.
back   **bag**

3.
rack   **rag**

8.
duck   **dug**

4.
puck   **pug**

9.
wick   **wig**

5.
pick   **pig**

10.
Matt   **mad**

_____ _____ _____

Name   Date   Homework Partner

Postvocalic Devoicing Word Level

#BK-320 Webber® Photo Phonology Minimal Pair Cards Fun Sheets • ©2005 Super Duper® Publications • www.superduperinc.com • 1-800-277-8737

Minimal Contrast Pairs

Directions: Have student point to picture-words as teacher/helper says each word aloud.

1. write   ride

2. sat   sad

3. seat   seed

4. lit   lid

5. bus   buzz

6. ice   eyes

7. fuss   fuzz

8. niece   knees

9. race   raise

10. rice   rise

_____   _____   _____

Name   Date   Homework Partner

#BK-320 Webber® Photo Phonology Minimal Pair Cards Fun Sheets • ©2005 Super Duper® Publications • www.superduperinc.com • 1-800-277-8737

157

Minimal Contrast Pairs

Directions: Have student point to picture-words as teacher/helper says each word aloud.

1. piece   peas

6. rip   rib

2. rope   robe

7. safe   save

3. cop   cob

8. leaf   leave

4. cup   cub

9. tack   tag

5. lap   lab

10. bus   buzz

_____ _____ _____

Name   Date   Homework Partner

Postvocalic Devoicing Word Level

#BK-320 Webber® Photo Phonology Minimal Pair Cards Fun Sheets • ©2005 Super Duper® Publications • www.superduperinc.com • 1-800-277-8737

Minimal Contrast Definitions

Directions: Read each question and possible answers aloud. Ask students to circle and/or say the correct answer.

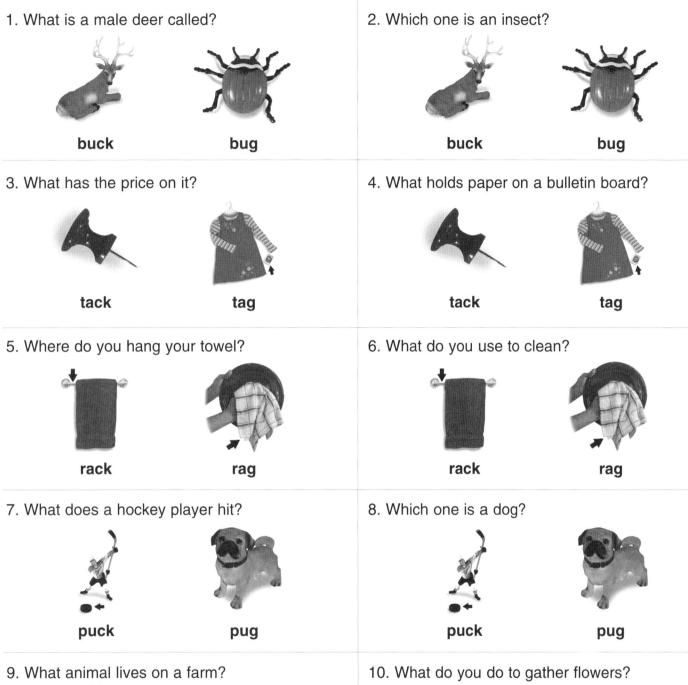

1. What is a male deer called?

buck   **bug**

2. Which one is an insect?

buck   **bug**

3. What has the price on it?

tack   **tag**

4. What holds paper on a bulletin board?

tack   **tag**

5. Where do you hang your towel?

rack   **rag**

6. What do you use to clean?

rack   **rag**

7. What does a hockey player hit?

puck   **pug**

8. Which one is a dog?

puck   **pug**

9. What animal lives on a farm?

pick   **pig**

10. What do you do to gather flowers?

pick   **pig**

_____ _____ _____
Name   Date   Homework Partner

Postvocalic Devoicing Word Level

Minimal Contrast Definitions

Directions: Read each question and possible answers aloud. Ask students to circle and/or say the correct answer.

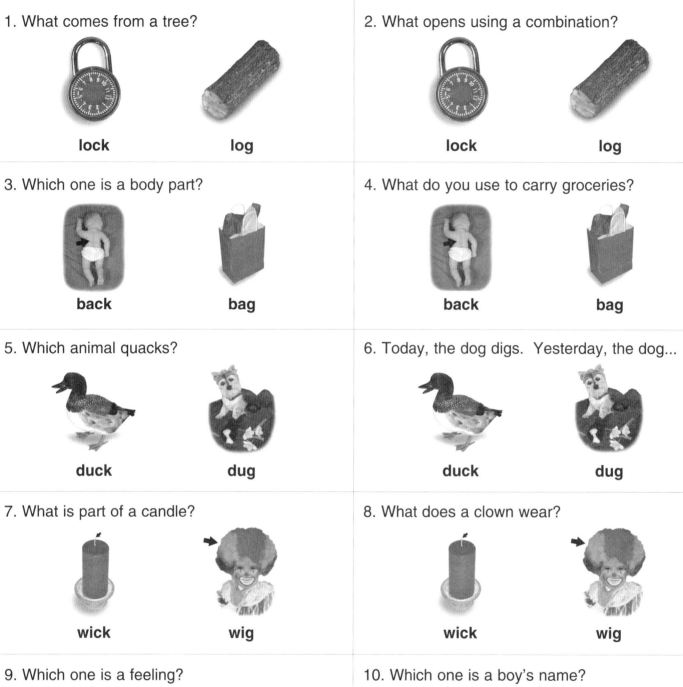

1. What comes from a tree?

lock   **log**

2. What opens using a combination?

lock   **log**

3. Which one is a body part?

back   **bag**

4. What do you use to carry groceries?

back   **bag**

5. Which animal quacks?

duck   **dug**

6. Today, the dog digs. Yesterday, the dog...

duck   **dug**

7. What is part of a candle?

wick   **wig**

8. What does a clown wear?

wick   **wig**

9. Which one is a feeling?

Matt   **mad**

10. Which one is a boy's name?

Matt   **mad**

_____   _____   _____

Name   Date   Homework Partner

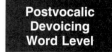
Postvocalic Devoicing Word Level

Minimal Contrast Definitions

Directions: Read each question and possible answers aloud. Ask students to circle and/or say the correct answer.

1. What do you do on a bike?

    write   **ride**

2. What do you do with a pencil?

    write   **ride**

3. What is the opposite of "stood"?

    sat   **sad**

4. How do you feel when you are upset?

    sat   **sad**

5. Where do you sit?

    seat   **seed**

6. What do you plant?

    seat   **seed**

7. What goes on a jar?

    lit   **lid**

8. What did someone do to the candles?

    lit   **lid**

9. What noise does a bee make?

    bus   **buzz**

10. What do you ride to school?

    bus   **buzz**

_____   _____   _____

Name   Date   Homework Partner

Minimal Contrast Definitions

Directions: Read each question and possible answers aloud. Ask students to circle and/or say the correct answer.

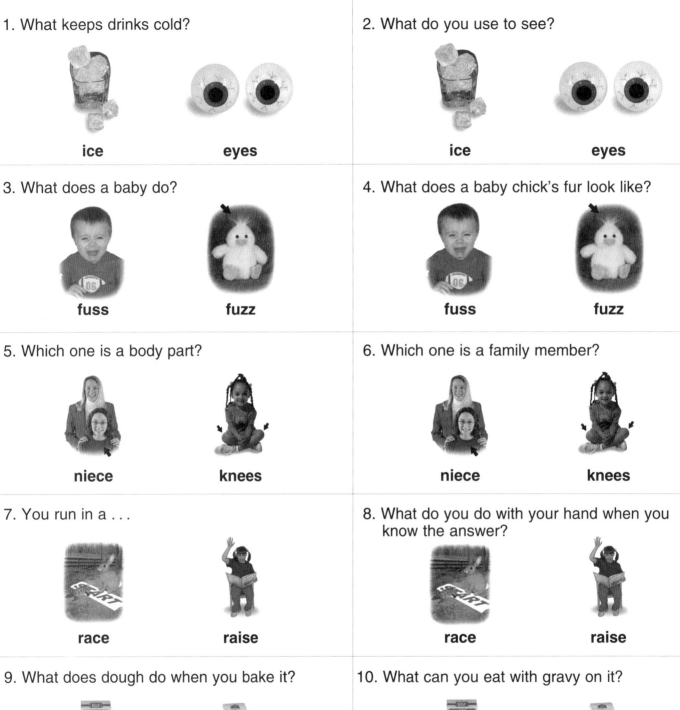

1. What keeps drinks cold?

    ice   **eyes**

2. What do you use to see?

    ice   **eyes**

3. What does a baby do?

    fuss   **fuzz**

4. What does a baby chick's fur look like?

    fuss   **fuzz**

5. Which one is a body part?

    niece   **knees**

6. Which one is a family member?

    niece   **knees**

7. You run in a . . .

    race   **raise**

8. What do you do with your hand when you know the answer?

    race   **raise**

9. What does dough do when you bake it?

    rice   **rise**

10. What can you eat with gravy on it?

    rice   **rise**

_____   _____   _____
 Name   Date   Homework Partner

Postvocalic Devoicing Word Level

#BK-320 Webber® Photo Phonology Minimal Pair Cards Fun Sheets • ©2005 Super Duper® Publications • www.superduperinc.com • 1-800-277-8737

Minimal Contrast Definitions

Directions: Read each question and possible answers aloud. Ask students to circle and/or say the correct answer.

1. Which one is a vegetable?

   piece   **peas**

2. I want some pie. Could I have a . . .?

   piece   **peas**

3. What do you wear?

   rope   **robe**

4. What do you use to tie things?

   rope   **robe**

5. Who helps people?

   cop   **cob**

6. Corn grows on a . . .

   cop   **cob**

7. What is a baby tiger called?

   cup   **cub**

8. What holds drinks?

   cup   **cub**

9. You can sit in your mother's . . .

   lap   **lab**

10. Which one is a dog?

   lap   **lab**

_____   _____   _____
Name   Date   Homework Partner

Postvocalic Devoicing Word Level

Minimal Contrast Definitions

Directions: Read each question and possible answers aloud. Ask students to circle and/or say the correct answer.

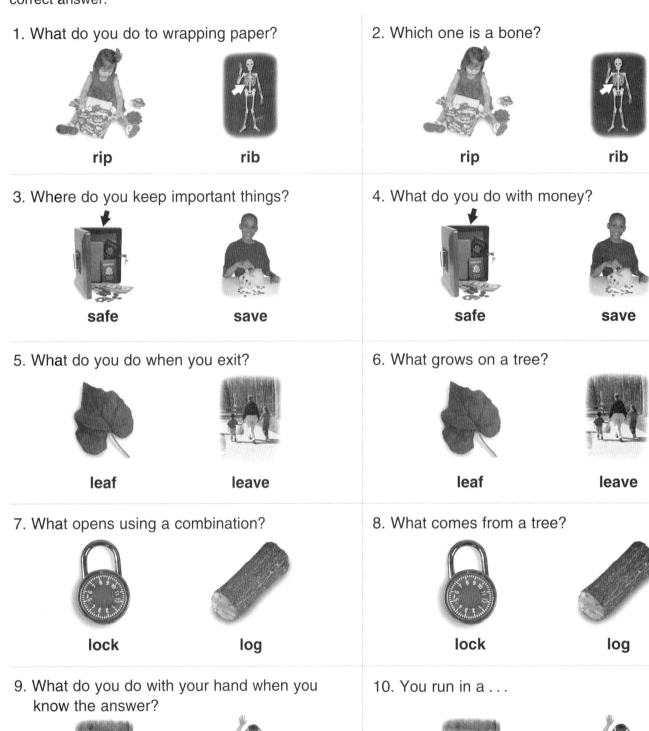

1. What do you do to wrapping paper?

    rip   **rib**

2. Which one is a bone?

    rip   **rib**

3. Where do you keep important things?

    safe   **save**

4. What do you do with money?

    safe   **save**

5. What do you do when you exit?

    leaf   **leave**

6. What grows on a tree?

    leaf   **leave**

7. What opens using a combination?

    lock   **log**

8. What comes from a tree?

    lock   **log**

9. What do you do with your hand when you know the answer?

    race   **raise**

10. You run in a . . .

    race   **raise**

_____   _____   _____
        Name   Date   Homework Partner

Postvocalic Devoicing Word Level

#BK-320 Webber® Photo Phonology Minimal Pair Cards Fun Sheets • ©2005 Super Duper® Publications • www.superduperinc.com • 1-800-277-8737

Fruit Basket

Directions: Cut out the fruit cards and place them face down in a pile. Turn over a card and read/say aloud the picture-word on the fruit as you glue, tape, or place the fruit into or around the basket.

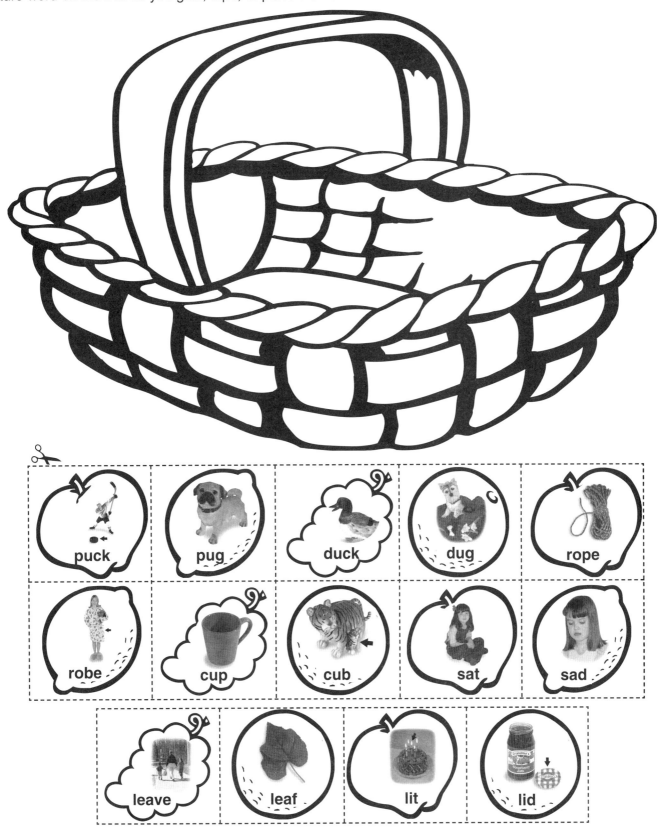

puck	pug	duck	dug	rope
robe	cup	cub	sat	sad

leave	leaf	lit	lid

_____   _____   _____
Name   Date   Homework Partner

Eggstravaganza

Directions: Read/say aloud the picture-words below. Then, cut out the markers. Begin at Start and flip a coin (heads=1, tails=2) to determine how many spaces to move. As you move, read/say each picture-word aloud. First player to reach the finish wins.

166   #BK-320 Webber® Photo Phonology Minimal Pair Cards Fun Sheets • ©2005 Super Duper® Publications • www.superduperinc.com • 1-800-277-8737

Name _____ Date _____ Homework Partner _____

Postvocalic Devoicing Word Level

Buzz Words

Directions: Read/say aloud the picture-words on each flower below. Circle the flower in each pair containing the word with a Z sound. Read/say the words aloud.

1. buzz / bus

4. rice / rise

2. ice / eyes

5. fuzz / fuss

3. peas / piece

6. race / raise

Name _____   Date _____   Homework Partner _____

Save a Penny

Directions: Cut out the coins below and place them face down in a pile. Choose a coin and read/say aloud the picture-word on it as you glue, tape, or place the coin onto the bank.

buck   bug   tack   tag   back   bag   Matt

mad   write   ride   lap   lab   rip   rib

_____   _____   _____

Name   Date   Homework Partner

Postvocalic Devoicing Word Level

#BK-320 Webber® Photo Phonology Minimal Pair Cards Fun Sheets • ©2005 Super Duper® Publications • www.superduperinc.com • 1-800-277-8737

Phrase Racing

Directions: Cut out a car for each player and put at the starting line. Flip a coin to determine how many spaces to move (heads=2, tails=1). Read/say aloud each phrase as you land on it. First one to the Finish wins!

START   START

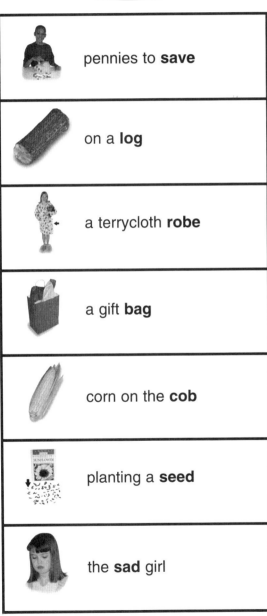

	pennies to **save**
	on a **log**
	a terrycloth **robe**
	a gift **bag**
	corn on the **cob**
	planting a **seed**
	the **sad** girl

	a gift **bag**
	corn on the **cob**
	the **sad** girl
	pennies to **save**
	planting a **seed**
	on a **log**
	a terrycloth **robe**

FINISH   FINISH

_____   _____   _____
Name   Date   Homework Partner

Postvocalic Devoicing Phrase Level

#BK-320 Webber® Photo Phonology Minimal Pair Cards Fun Sheets • ©2005 Super Duper® Publications • www.superduperinc.com • 1-800-277-8737

169

Go-Together Match-Ups

Directions: Draw a line from the words in Column A to the word that goes with it in Column B. Read/say each phrase aloud *("a curly wig")*.

A

a curly

jar and

little tiger

nose and

old price

a loud

B

lid

tag

buzz

eyes

wig

cub

#BK-320 Webber® Photo Phonology Minimal Pair Cards Fun Sheets • ©2005 Super Duper® Publications • www.superduperinc.com • 1-800-277-8737

Name   Date   Homework Partner

Postvocalic Devoicing Phrase Level

Puzzle Match

Directions: Draw a line from a puzzle piece in Column A to the one that matches it in Column B. Read/say the phrases aloud.

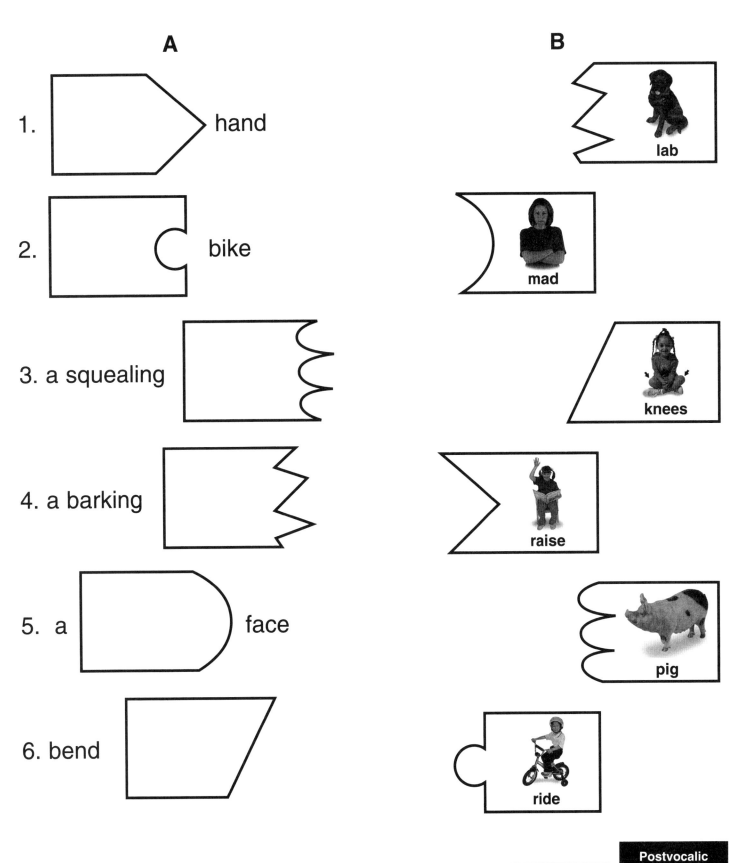

A

1. hand

2. bike

3. a squealing

4. a barking

5. a ⌂ face

6. bend

B

lab

mad

knees

raise

pig

ride

Postvocalic Devoicing Phrase Level

Mine or Yours?

Directions: Read/say each picture-word below. Cut out the pictures and put face down in a pile. Turn over a picture and flip a coin. Heads means you keep the picture and say, *"my _____"* (*"my shape"*). Tails means you give the picture to your partner and say, *"your _____"* (*"your shape"*). Most pictures at the end wins.

buck	**bug**	**duck**	**dug**
rack	**rag**	**fuss**	**fuzz**
rice	**rise**	**rip**	**rib**
leaf	**leave**	**safe**	**save**
bus	**buzz**	**lock**	**log**

_____ _____ _____

Name   Date   Homework Partner

Postvocalic Devoicing Phrase Level

#BK-320 Webber® Photo Phonology Minimal Pair Cards Fun Sheets • ©2005 Super Duper® Publications • www.superduperinc.com • 1-800-277-8737

"I would..."

Directions: Read/say the questions below. Answer each question, using the target word in a sentence. *(Example: "If I planted a magic seed, a magic tree would grow.")*

1. If you could your money, what would you buy?

   save

2. If you had a , what would you teach it to do?

   pug

3. If you found a mysterious , what would be inside?

   bag

4. If you had to eat , what would you do?

   peas

5. If you planted a magic , what would grow?

   seed

6. If your friend was , what would you say?

   sad

7. If you found a , where would you take it?

   cub

_____ _____ _____

Name   Date   Homework Partner

Postvocalic Devoicing Sentence Level

Replace It

Directions: Read/say each sentence below. Change the underlined word in the sentence so that it makes sense using a picture-word from the Word Bank. Then, read/say the corrected sentence aloud.

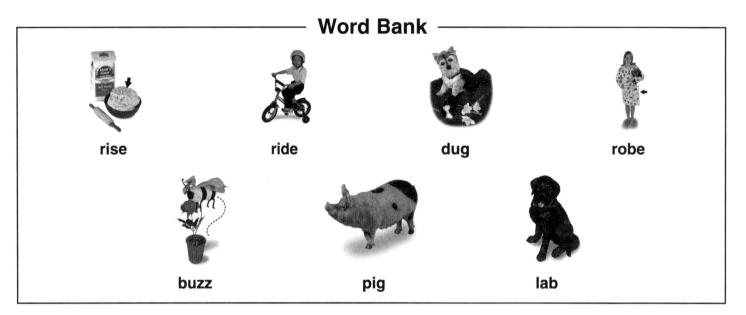

Word Bank

rise   ride   dug   robe

buzz   pig   lab

1. Go <u>kiss</u> your bike.

2. Listen to the barking <u>elephant</u>.

3. Hang your <u>shoes</u> in the bathroom.

4. The bees will <u>meow.</u>

5. The dog <u>rolled</u> up a bone.

6. The dough needs to <u>jump</u>.

7. A <u>mouse</u> says *"oink oink."*

Answer Key: 1. ride 2. lab 3. robe 4. buzz 5. dug 6. rise 7. pig

Postvocalic
Devoicing
Sentence Level

Name   Date   Homework Partner

One, Two, Three

Directions: Each student gets three turns to roll the die. The number on the die corresponds to the number next to the phrase to be used in a silly sentence. For example, a student who rolls a two, five, and one will make a sentence with the phrases: *"The spider will close the zoo soon."*

	Roll One	Roll Two	Roll Three
	1. The family	will leave	the zoo soon.
	2. The spider	will catch	the bug.
	3. The clown	will wear	a wig.
	4. Grandma	will open	the lid on the jar.
	5. The baby	will close	her eyes.
	6. The student	will raise	her hand.

_____ _____ _____

Name   Date   Homework Partner

Spin a Sentence

Directions: Read/say aloud the picture-words below. If you prefer, glue this page to construction paper for added durability. Cut out the arrow/dial. Use a brad to connect the dial to the circle. Spin the spinner. When you land on a sentence, complete the sentence by choosing the correct picture-word. Read/say the sentence aloud.

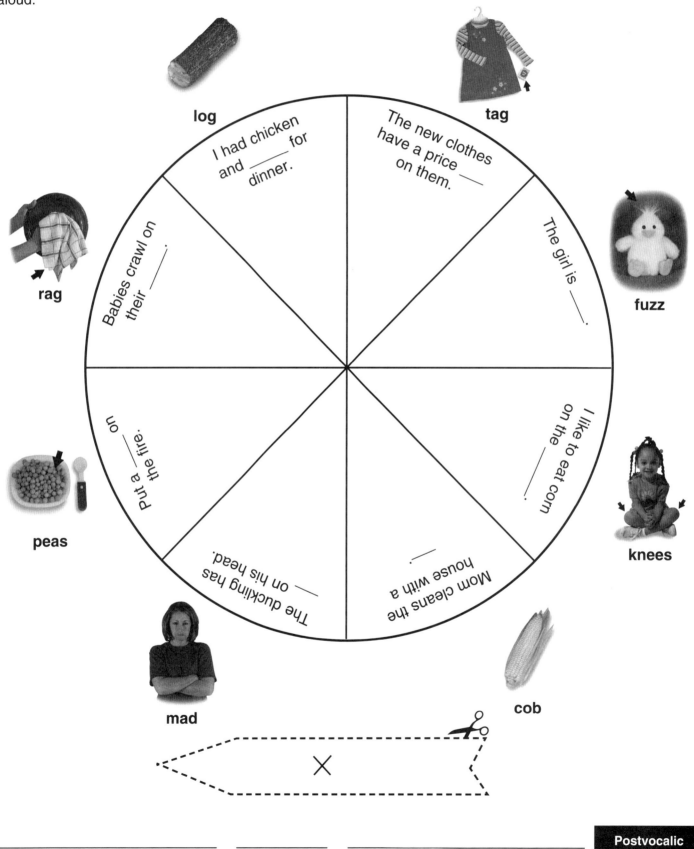

log

tag

rag

I had chicken and _____ for dinner.

The new clothes have a price _____ on them.

Babies crawl on their _____.

The girl is _____.

fuzz

Put a _____ on the fire.

I like to eat corn on the _____.

peas

knees

The duckling has _____ on his head.

Mom cleans the house with a _____.

mad

cob

Name _____ Date _____ Homework Partner _____

Postvocalic Devoicing Sentence Level

Auditory Bombardment

Directions: Have the student listen carefully as you read the following list of words slowly and clearly. The student does not need to repeat the words, but just listen to them. You may have the student engage in a quiet activity, like coloring, as you read.

1. bed	34. vote	67. girl
2. boat	35. vest	68. gang
3. bell	36. vent	69. golf
4. boil	37. vine	70. goose
5. box	38. dice	71. gum
6. bill	39. deer	72. gift
7. bark	40. dad	73. chart
8. bulb	41. door	74. chin
9. bus	42. dime	75. chair
10. burn	43. dove	76. chalk
11. pie	44. dirt	77. chip
12. pill	45. ditch	78. chew
13. pour	46. dock	79. chop
14. pants	47. cup	80. change
15. pitch	48. cape	81. leg
16. page	49. cake	82. lace
17. pool	50. cough	83. lamp
18. paint	51. coat	84. light
19. push	52. coal	85. lip
20. part	53. cage	86. lucky
21. feet	54. cook	87. line
22. fall	55. comb	88. leash
23. farm	56. tacks	89. sink
24. fear	57. tear	90. saw
25. fish	58. ten	91. soap
26. phone	59. toad	92. yawn
27. four	60. time	93. year
28. fan	61. tart	94. young
29. fast	62. tire	95. yard
30. food	63. type	96. howl
31. vase	64. toy	97. heel
32. voice	65. game	98. hole
33. van	66. gold	99. hat
		100. house

_____   _____   _____

Name   Date   Homework Partner

Initial Consonant Deletion Word Level

Minimal Contrast Pairs

Directions: Have student point to picture-words as teacher/helper says each word aloud.

1.
Ed   bed

2.
oat   boat

3.
L   bell

4.
oil   boil

5.
eye   pie

6.
ill   pill

7.
oar   pour

8.
ants   pants

9.
eat   feet

10.
all   fall

_____ _____ _____

Name   Date   Homework Partner

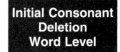

Initial Consonant Deletion Word Level

#BK-320 Webber® Photo Phonology Minimal Pair Cards Fun Sheets • ©2005 Super Duper® Publications • www.superduperinc.com • 1-800-277-8737

Minimal Contrast Pairs

Directions: Have student point to picture-words as teacher/helper says each word aloud.

1.

arm   **farm**

2.

ace   **vase**

3.

ice   **dice**

4.

ear   **deer**

5.

add   **dad**

6.

up   **cup**

7.

ape   **cape**

8.

ache   **cake**

9.

off   **cough**

10.

oat   **boat**

_____   _____   _____
Name   Date   Homework Partner

Minimal Contrast Pairs

Directions: Have student point to picture-words as teacher/helper says each word aloud.

1. ax   tacks

2. aim   game

3. old   gold

4. art   chart

5. in   chin

6. egg   leg

7. ink   sink

8. on   yawn

9. owl   howl

10. oar   pour

_____   _____   _____

Name   Date   Homework Partner

Initial Consonant Deletion Word Level

#BK-320 Webber® Photo Phonology Minimal Pair Cards Fun Sheets • ©2005 Super Duper® Publications • www.superduperinc.com • 1-800-277-8737

Minimal Contrast Definitions

Directions: Read each question and possible answers aloud. Ask students to circle and/or say the correct answer.

1. Where do you sleep?

Ed   **bed**

2. Which one is a boy's name?

Ed   **bed**

3. Which one grows and is used for food?

oat   **boat**

4. What floats on water?

oat   **boat**

5. Which one is a letter?

L   **bell**

6. What rings?

L   **bell**

7. What can hot water do?

oil   **boil**

8. What do you put in food?

oil   **boil**

9. What do you eat?

eye   **pie**

10. What do you use to see?

eye   **pie**

_____ _____ _____

Name   Date   Homework Partner

Initial Consonant Deletion Word Level

Minimal Contrast Definitions

Directions: Read each question and possible answers aloud. Ask students to circle and/or say the correct answer.

1. How do you feel when you are sick?

ill   pill

2. What do you swallow?

ill   pill

3. What do you do with juice in a pitcher?

oar   pour

4. What do you use to paddle?

oar   pour

5. What do you wear?

ants   pants

6. What lives in the ground?

ants   pants

7. What do you do with food?

eat   feet

8. Which one is a body part?

eat   feet

9. One dog has none. The other dog has...

all   fall

10. Which one is a season?

all   fall

_____ _____ _____

Name   Date   Homework Partner

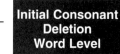

Initial Consonant Deletion Word Level

#BK-320 Webber® Photo Phonology Minimal Pair Cards Fun Sheets • ©2005 Super Duper® Publications • www.superduperinc.com • 1-800-277-8737

Minimal Contrast Definitions

Directions: Read each question and possible answers aloud. Ask students to circle and/or say the correct answer.

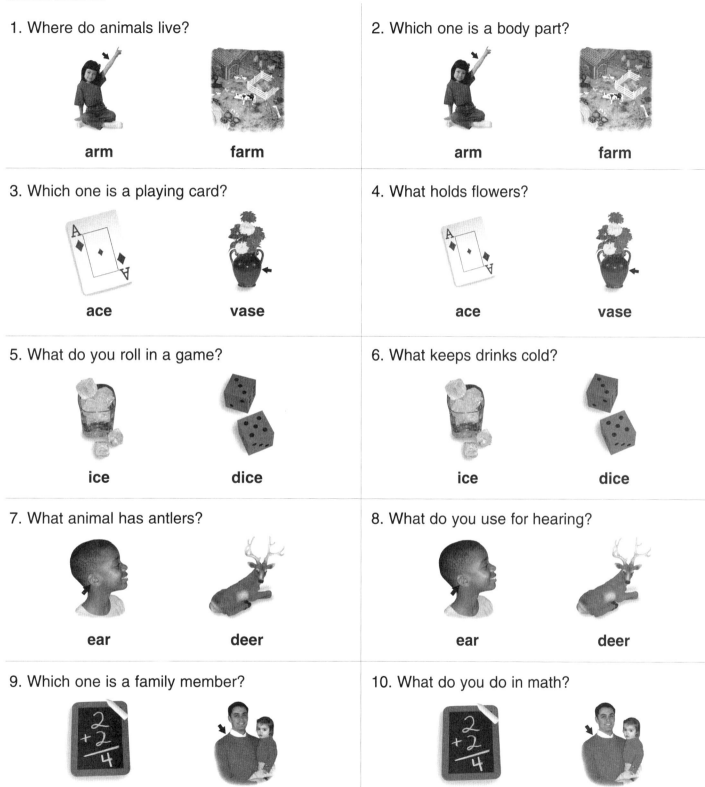

1. Where do animals live?

    arm   **farm**

2. Which one is a body part?

    arm   **farm**

3. Which one is a playing card?

    ace   **vase**

4. What holds flowers?

    ace   **vase**

5. What do you roll in a game?

    ice   **dice**

6. What keeps drinks cold?

    ice   **dice**

7. What animal has antlers?

    ear   **deer**

8. What do you use for hearing?

    ear   **deer**

9. Which one is a family member?

    add   **dad**

10. What do you do in math?

    add   **dad**

_____ _____ _____

Name   Date   Homework Partner

Initial Consonant Deletion Word Level

Minimal Contrast Definitions

Directions: Read each question and possible answers aloud. Ask students to circle and/or say the correct answer.

1. What is the opposite of "down"?

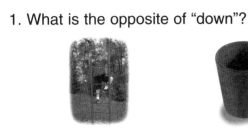

up   **cup**

2. What do you use for drinking?

up   **cup**

3. Which one is an animal?

ape   **cape**

4. What does a superhero wear?

ape   **cape**

5. What can you eat that has frosting?

ache   **cake**

6. What do you feel when you are in pain?

ache   **cake**

7. What is the opposite of "on"?

off   **cough**

8. What do you do when you are sick?

off   **cough**

9. What holds paper on a bulletin board?

ax   **tacks**

10. Which one is a tool?

ax   **tacks**

Initial Consonant
Deletion
Word Level

_____   _____   _____
Name   Date   Homework Partner

#BK-320 Webber® Photo Phonology Minimal Pair Cards Fun Sheets • ©2005 Super Duper® Publications • www.superduperinc.com • 1-800-277-8737

Minimal Contrast Definitions

Directions: Read each question and possible answers aloud. Ask students to circle and/or say the correct answer.

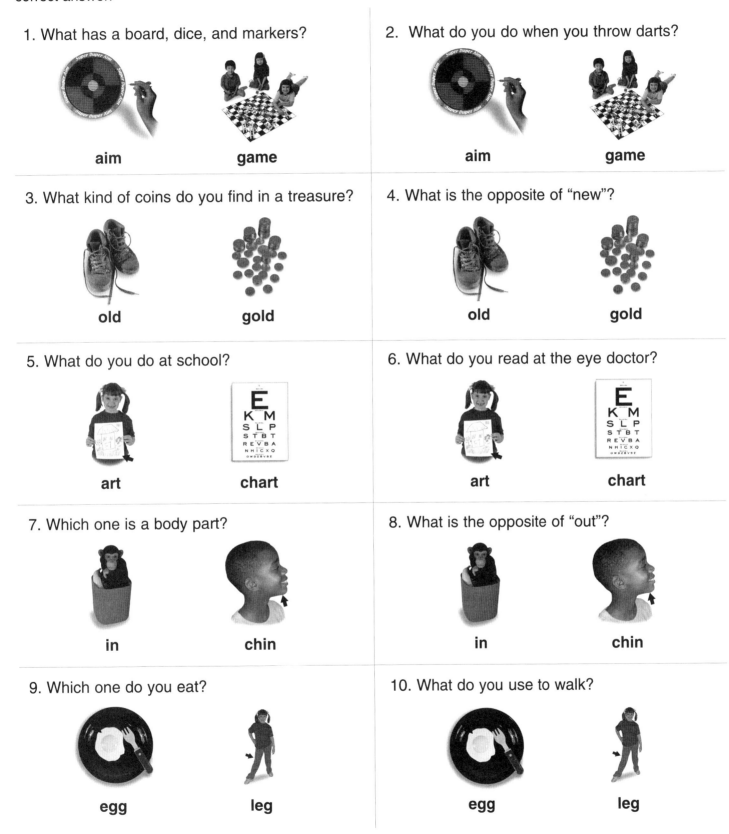

1. What has a board, dice, and markers?

aim   **game**

2. What do you do when you throw darts?

aim   **game**

3. What kind of coins do you find in a treasure?

old   **gold**

4. What is the opposite of "new"?

old   **gold**

5. What do you do at school?

art   **chart**

6. What do you read at the eye doctor?

art   **chart**

7. Which one is a body part?

in   **chin**

8. What is the opposite of "out"?

in   **chin**

9. Which one do you eat?

egg   **leg**

10. What do you use to walk?

egg   **leg**

_____   _____   _____

Name   Date   Homework Partner

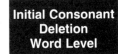

Initial Consonant
Deletion
Word Level

Minimal Contrast Definitions

Directions: Read each question and possible answers aloud. Ask students to circle and/or say the correct answer.

1. What is in a pen?

ink   **sink**

2. Where do you wash your hands?

ink   **sink**

3. What is the opposite of "off"?

on   **yawn**

4. What do you do when you are sleepy?

on   **yawn**

5. What does a wolf do?

owl   **howl**

6. What flies?

owl   **howl**

7. What do you use for drinking?

up   **cup**

8. What is the opposite of "down"?

up   **cup**

9. What rings?

L   **bell**

10. Which one is a letter?

L   **bell**

_____ _____ _____

Name   Date   Homework Partner

#BK-320 Webber® Photo Phonology Minimal Pair Cards Fun Sheets • ©2005 Super Duper® Publications • www.superduperinc.com • 1-800-277-8737

Time for Pie

Directions: Cut out the pies below. Read/say each picture-word as you glue, tape, or place each one onto the baker's shelf.

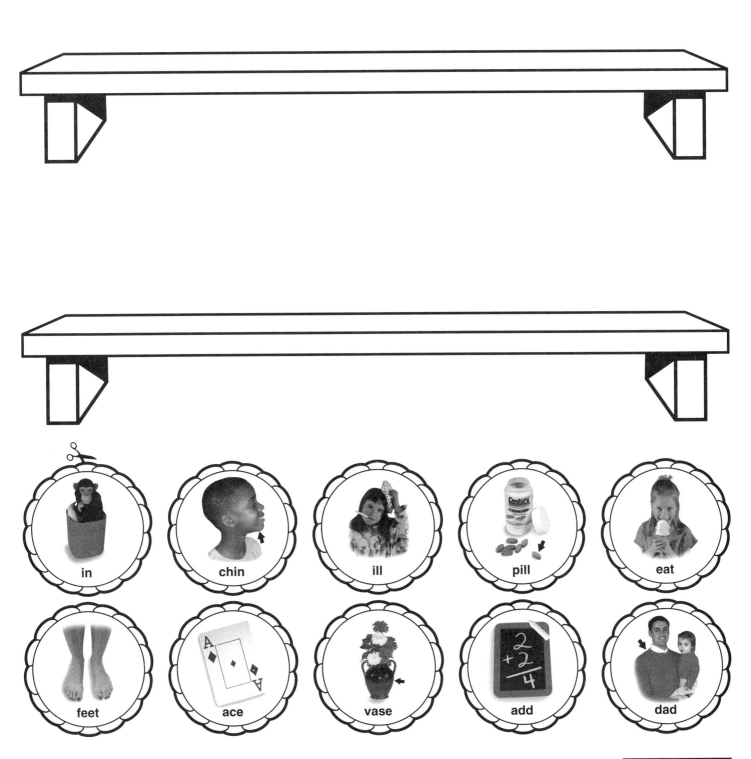

in

chin

ill

pill

eat

feet

ace

vase

add

dad

_____ _____ _____

Name   Date   Homework Partner

Memory Game

Directions: Read/say aloud each picture-word below. Cut out the pictures. Place all cards face down. Turn over cards two at a time and try to find a match. Say each card as you pick it up. Keep all matches. Most matches wins!

oat	boat	eye	pie
oar	pour	all	fall
ice	dice	oat	boat
eye	pie	oar	pour
all	fall	ice	dice

Name   Date   Homework Partner

#BK-320 Webber® Photo Phonology Minimal Pair Cards Fun Sheets • ©2005 Super Duper® Publications • www.superduperinc.com • 1-800-277-8737

Hide 'n' Seek

Directions: Read/say aloud the picture-words. Cut out the pictures and penny. Place the pictures face up. Teacher/helper hides the penny under a picture. Say each picture-word as you look underneath for the penny. Find the penny and you win!

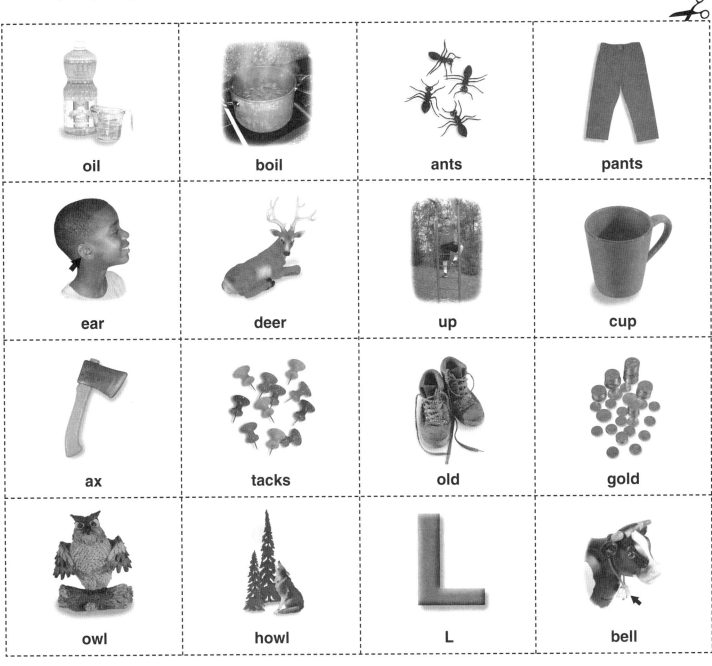

oil	boil	ants	pants
ear	deer	up	cup
ax	tacks	old	gold
owl	howl	L	bell

_____ _____ _____
Name   Date   Homework Partner

Initial Consonant Deletion Word Level

Bath Fun

Directions: Cut out the bubbles below. Read/say each picture-word as you glue, tape, or place each one in or around the bathtub.

Ed   bed   arm   farm   ape   cape   ache

cake   off   cough   egg   leg   on   yawn

_____ _____ _____

Name   Date   Homework Partner

Initial Consonant Deletion Word Level

#BK-320 Webber® Photo Phonology Minimal Pair Cards Fun Sheets • ©2005 Super Duper® Publications • www.superduperinc.com • 1-800-277-8737

X and O

Directions: Cut out each X and O below. Have each player/partner choose X or O. The first player reads/ says a picture-word aloud and places an X or O on the square. Play continues in turn. The first person to get three in a row wins.

the ringing bell	winning the game	a big yawn
a pair of pants	pour juice	a superhero's cape
rolling the dice	an eye chart	a wedding cake

_____ _____ _____

Name · Date · Homework Partner

Letter Shuffle

Directions: Read/say aloud the picture–words. Then, unscramble the letters in parenthesis after each phrase. (Scrambled words are the same as picture-words.) Write the word in the blank space. Read/say each phrase.

gold

sink

1. a toy _____ (taob)

2. mom and _____ (add)

3. the kitchen _____ (nski)

fall

4. _____ and ice cream (ipe)

dad

5. a pot of _____ (oldg)

6. winter, spring, summer, and _____ (flal)

boat

pie

Answer Key: 1. boat 2. dad 3. sink 4. pie 5. gold 6. fall

_____ _____ _____

Name   Date   Homework Partner

#BK-320 Webber® Photo Phonology Minimal Pair Cards Fun Sheets • ©2005 Super Duper® Publications • www.superduperinc.com • 1-800-277-8737

Fold Again

Directions: Fold this page along the dotted lines so that the arrows at the top meet. Read/say aloud the phrases you see using the describing word and the picture-word *("a broken vase")*.

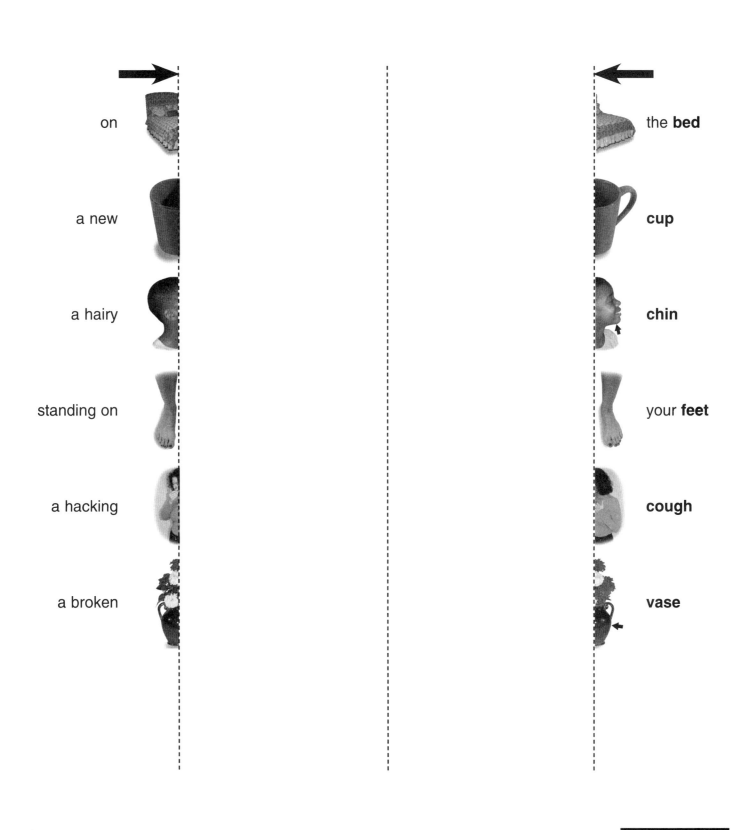

on · · · the **bed**

a new · · · **cup**

a hairy · · · **chin**

standing on · · · your **feet**

a hacking · · · **cough**

a broken · · · **vase**

_____ _____ _____

Name   Date   Homework Partner

#BK-320 Webber® Photo Phonology Minimal Pair Cards Fun Sheets • ©2005 Super Duper® Publications • www.superduperinc.com • 1-800-277-8737

Heads or Tails

Directions: Cut out the cards below. Place them in a pile face down. Turn over a card and flip a coin. Heads means to use the picture-word in the phrase *"big _____."* Tails means to use the picture-word in the phrase *"little _____."*

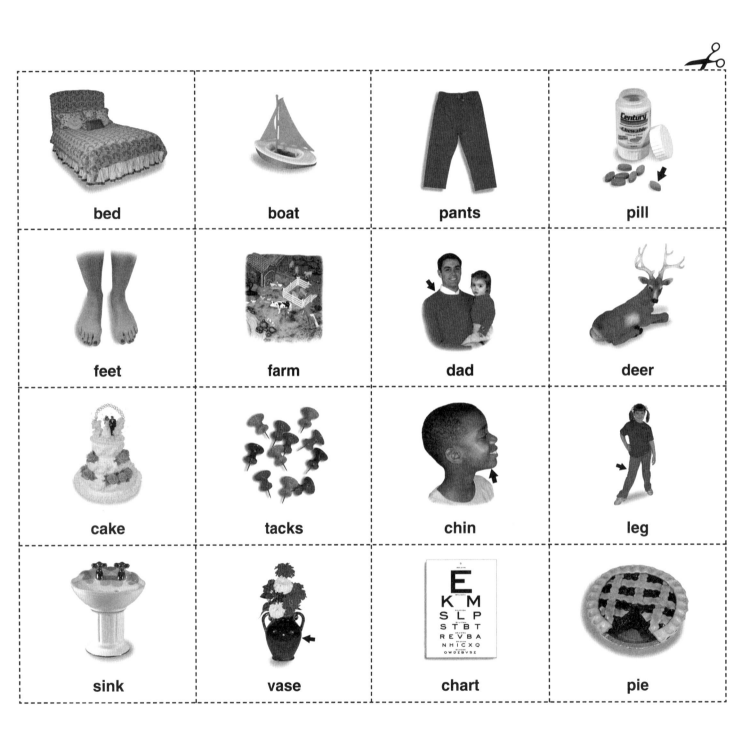

bed	boat	pants	pill
feet	farm	dad	deer
cake	tacks	chin	leg
sink	vase	chart	pie

_____ _____ _____

Name　　　　　　　　　　　Date　　　　　　　　Homework Partner

#BK-320 Webber® Photo Phonology Minimal Pair Cards Fun Sheets • ©2005 Super Duper® Publications • www.superduperinc.com • 1-800-277-8737

Sentence Fill-In

Directions: Draw a line from the sentence in Column A to the picture-word that completes it in Column B.

A

1. The pirate found _____ in the treasure.

2. Please _____ the lemonade.

3. The girl went to the doctor for her _____.

4. At night, the wolves _____.

5. _____ some water on the stove.

6. Let's play a board _____.

7. My _____ likes watching sports.

B

game

cough

boil

gold

dad

pour

howl

_____   _____   _____
Name   Date   Homework Partner

Replace It

Directions: Read/say each sentence below. Using a picture-word from the Word Bank, change the underlined word in the sentence so that it makes sense. Then, read/say the corrected sentence aloud.

Word Bank

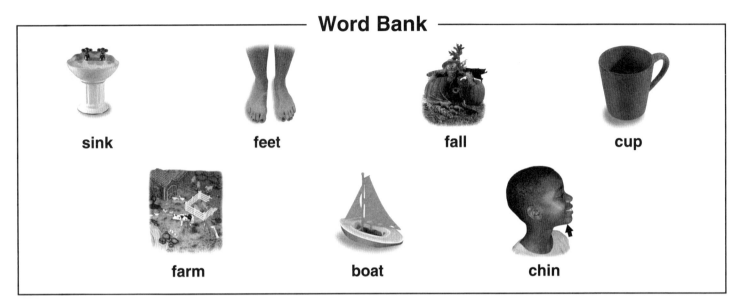

sink   feet   fall   cup

farm   boat   chin

1. The family went sailing on the <u>bike</u>.

2. The child put sandals on his <u>ears</u>.

3. A pig is a <u>zoo</u> animal.

4. Pour my cocoa in a <u>sock</u>.

5. Your <u>elbow</u> is part of your face.

6. Wash your hands in the <u>toilet</u>.

7. The leaves turn yellow and orange in the <u>spring</u>.

Answer Key: 1. boat 2. feet 3. farm 4. cup 5. chin 6. sink 7. fall

_____ _____ _____

Name   Date   Homework Partner

Initial Consonant Deletion Sentence Level

One, Two, Three

Directions: Each student gets three turns to roll the die. The number on the die corresponds to the number next to the phrase to be used in a silly sentence. For example, a student who rolls a two, five, and one will make a sentence with the phrases: *"The dog buys tacks while tying his shoe."*

	Roll One	**Roll Two**	**Roll Three**
	1. The student	rings the bell	while tying his shoe.
	2. The dog	wears baseball pants	at camp.
	3. The player	rolls the dice	to see if he can eat.
	4. The monkey	wears a cape	to bed.
	5. The dancer	buys tacks	for dance class.
	6. The doctor	looks at the chart	during the movie.

_____   _____   _____
Name   Date   Homework Partner

Initial Consonant
Deletion
Sentence Level

Story Loop

Directions: Read/say aloud each picture-word. Make up a story using all of the pictures in the circle. You can start anywhere in the circle and go in either direction, but you must always end where you started to complete the loop. Say your story aloud.

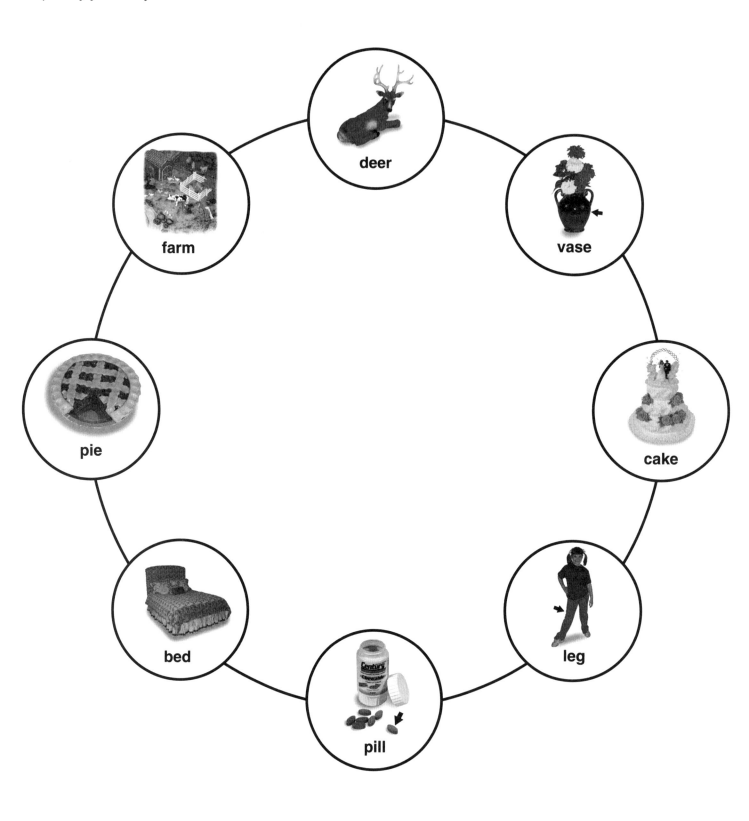

#BK-320 Webber® Photo Phonology Minimal Pair Cards Fun Sheets • ©2005 Super Duper® Publications • www.superduperinc.com • 1-800-277-8737

Auditory Bombardment

Directions: Have the student listen carefully as you read the following list of words slowly and clearly. The student does not need to repeat the words, but just listen to them. You may have the student engage in a quiet activity, like coloring, as you read.

1. dock	34. grade	67. bass
2. dot	35. head	68. bell
3. dice	36. kid	69. back
4. deer	37. lad	70. bulb
5. dine	38. wood	71. buzz
6. day	39. thread	72. boy
7. deck	40. slide	73. box
8. dough	41. sled	74. boat
9. does	42. shed	75. bird
10. dad	43. red	76. sub
11. dove	44. sand	77. rib
12. duck	45. shade	78. bib
13. dish	46. dude	79. crab
14. deep	47. mud	80. cob
15. doll	48. pad	81. globe
16. door	49. read	82. scab
17. dig	50. seed	83. club
18. dirt	51. bead	84. cab
19. dorm	52. bear	85. fib
20. dust	53. ball	86. lobe
21. date	54. bat	87. cube
22. dance	55. bug	88. crib
23. desk	56. bake	89. tube
24. den	57. bath	90. web
25. dime	58. belt	91. tab
26. dog	59. bark	92. grab
27. crowd	60. bunny	93. tub
28. lead	61. bike	94. robe
29. bread	62. Ben	95. shrub
30. bride	63. boo	96. bribe
31. cloud	64. beg	97. job
32. feed	65. bud	98. knob
33. flood	66. beet	99. lab
		100. Rob

_____ _____ _____

Name   Date   Homework Partner

Minimal Contrast Pairs

Directions: Have student point to picture-words as teacher/helper says each word aloud.

1. knock — dock

2. knot — dot

3. nice — dice

4. near — deer

5. nine — dine

6. neigh — day

Neigh

7. neck — deck

8. no — dough

9. nose — does

10. melt — belt

_____   _____   _____

Name   Date   Homework Partner

#BK-320 Webber® Photo Phonology Minimal Pair Cards Fun Sheets • ©2005 Super Duper® Publications • www.superduperinc.com • 1-800-277-8737

Minimal Contrast Pairs

Directions: Have student point to picture-words as teacher/helper says each word aloud.

1. **crown** **crowd**

6. **mug** **bug**

2. **bean** **bead**

7. **make** **bake**

3. **mare** **bear**

8. **math** **bath**

4. **mall** **ball**

9. **melt** **belt**

5. **Matt** **bat**

10. **meat** **beet**

_____ _____ _____

Name   Date   Homework Partner

Nasalization Word Level

Minimal Contrast Pairs

Directions: Have student point to picture-words as teacher/helper says each word aloud.

1.	**Mark**	**bark**	6.	**Meg**	**beg**
2.	**money**	**bunny**	7.	**mud**	**bud**
3.	**Mike**	**bike**	8.	**meat**	**beet**
4.	**men**	**Ben**	9.	**sub**	**sum**
5.	**moo**	**boo**	10.	**rib**	**rim**

_____ _____ _____

Name   Date   Homework Partner

#BK-320 Webber® Photo Phonology Minimal Pair Cards Fun Sheets • ©2005 Super Duper® Publications • www.superduperinc.com • 1-800-277-8737

Minimal Contrast Definitions

Directions: Read each question and possible answers aloud. Ask students to circle and/or say the correct answer.

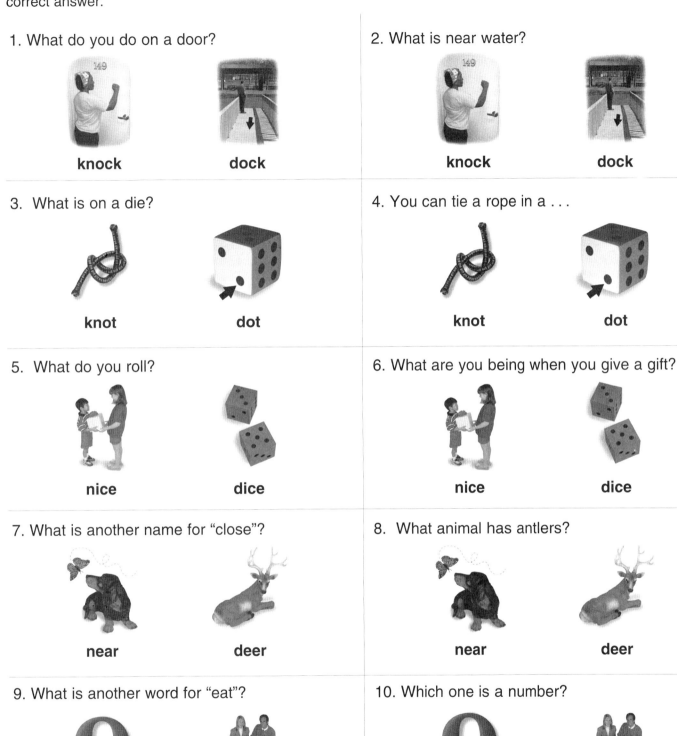

1. What do you do on a door?

knock   **dock**

2. What is near water?

knock   **dock**

3. What is on a die?

knot   **dot**

4. You can tie a rope in a . . .

knot   **dot**

5. What do you roll?

nice   **dice**

6. What are you being when you give a gift?

nice   **dice**

7. What is another name for "close"?

near   **deer**

8. What animal has antlers?

near   **deer**

9. What is another word for "eat"?

nine   **dine**

10. Which one is a number?

nine   **dine**

_____ _____ _____

Name   Date   Homework Partner

Nasalization Word Level

Minimal Contrast Definitions

Directions: Read each question and possible answers aloud. Ask students to circle and/or say the correct answer.

1. What is the opposite of "night"?

   neigh   **day**

2. What does a horse say?

   neigh   **day**

3. Which one is a body part?

   neck   **deck**

4. What do you call a pack of playing cards?

   neck   **deck**

5. What do you use to make cookies?

   no   **dough**

6. What is the opposite of "yes"?

   no   **dough**

7. Which one is a body part?

   nose   **does**

8. What do you call several female deer?

   nose   **does**

9. What does a queen wear?

   crown   **crowd**

10. What is a large group of people called?

    crown   **crowd**

_____   _____   _____
Name   Date   Homework Partner

#BK-320 Webber® Photo Phonology Minimal Pair Cards Fun Sheets • ©2005 Super Duper® Publications • www.superduperinc.com • 1-800-277-8737

Minimal Contrast Definitions

Directions: Read each question and possible answers aloud. Ask students to circle and/or say the correct answer.

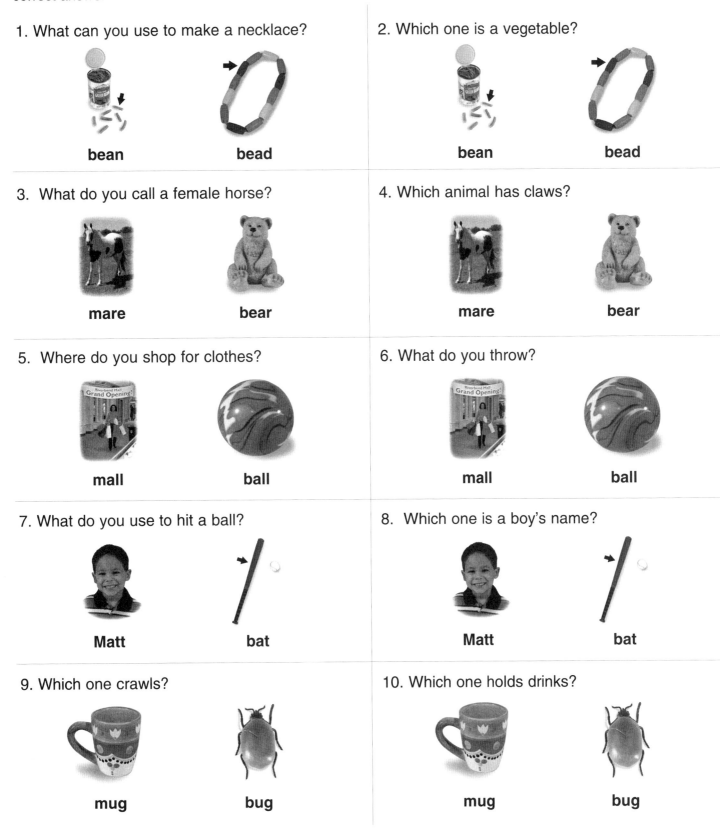

1. What can you use to make a necklace?

   bean   **bead**

2. Which one is a vegetable?

   bean   **bead**

3. What do you call a female horse?

   mare   **bear**

4. Which animal has claws?

   mare   **bear**

5. Where do you shop for clothes?

   mall   **ball**

6. What do you throw?

   mall   **ball**

7. What do you use to hit a ball?

   Matt   **bat**

8. Which one is a boy's name?

   Matt   **bat**

9. Which one crawls?

   mug   **bug**

10. Which one holds drinks?

   mug   **bug**

_____ _____ _____

Name   Date   Homework Partner

Nasalization Word Level

Minimal Contrast Definitions

Directions: Read each question and possible answers aloud. Ask students to circle and/or say the correct answer.

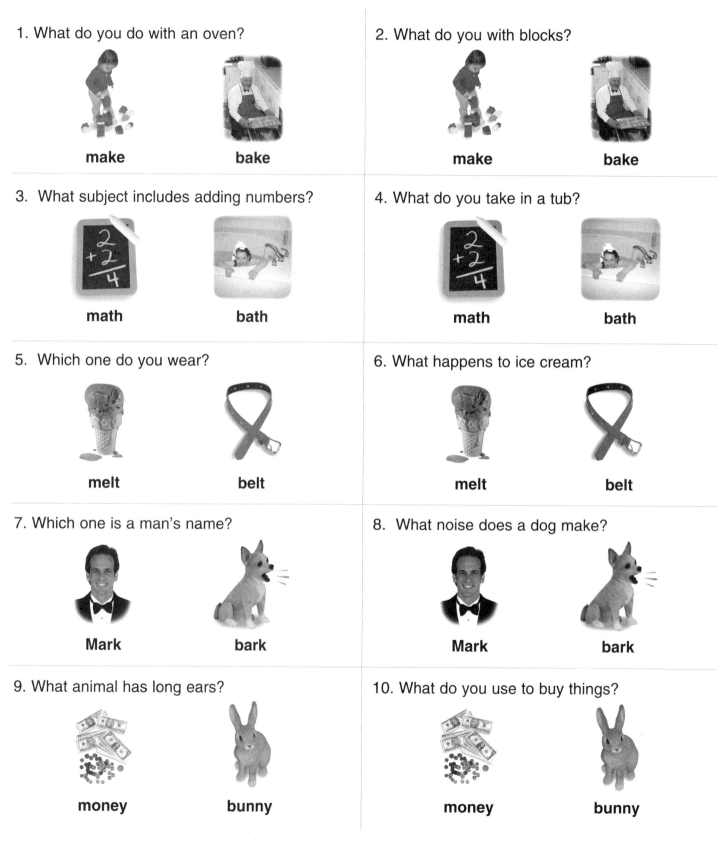

1. What do you do with an oven?

make   **bake**

2. What do you with blocks?

make   **bake**

3. What subject includes adding numbers?

math   **bath**

4. What do you take in a tub?

math   **bath**

5. Which one do you wear?

melt   **belt**

6. What happens to ice cream?

melt   **belt**

7. Which one is a man's name?

Mark   **bark**

8. What noise does a dog make?

Mark   **bark**

9. What animal has long ears?

money   **bunny**

10. What do you use to buy things?

money   **bunny**

_____   _____   _____

Name   Date   Homework Partner

Nasalization Word Level

Minimal Contrast Definitions

Directions: Read each question and possible answers aloud. Ask students to circle and/or say the correct answer.

1. Which one do you ride?

Mike   bike

2. Which one is a boy's name?

Mike   bike

3. What is a part of a basketball goal?

rib   rim

4. Which one is a bone?

rib   rim

5. What does a ghost say?

moo   boo

6. What does a cow say?

moo   boo

7. What does a dog do?

Meg   beg

8. Which one is a girl's name?

Meg   beg

9. What does a pig like?

mud   bud

10. What is a flower before it blooms?

mud   bud

_____ _____ _____

Name   Date   Homework Partner

Nasalization Word Level

Minimal Contrast Definitions

Directions: Read each question and possible answers aloud. Ask students to circle and/or say the correct answer.

1. Steak is a kind of . . .

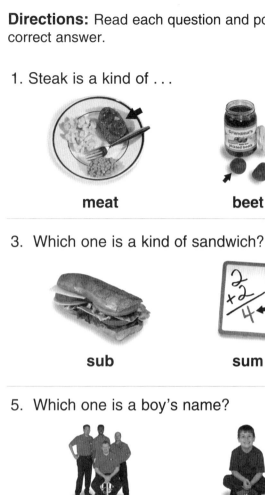

meat   **beet**

2. Which one is a vegetable?

meat   **beet**

3. Which one is a kind of sandwich?

sub   **sum**

4. What do you get when you add?

sub   **sum**

5. Which one is a boy's name?

men   **Ben**

6. What do you call more than one man?

men   **Ben**

7. What happens to ice cream?

melt   **belt**

8. Which one do you wear?

melt   **belt**

9. Which one is an animal with antlers?

near   **deer**

10. What is another name for "close"?

near   **deer**

_____   _____   _____

Name   Date   Homework Partner

#BK-320 Webber® Photo Phonology Minimal Pair Cards Fun Sheets • ©2005 Super Duper® Publications • www.superduperinc.com • 1-800-277-8737

Elly Elephant

Directions: Cut out the peanuts below and place them face down in a pile. Then, cut along the dotted line to make the elephants mouth. Turn over each card and read/say the picture-word as you feed the elephant.

near

mall

make

deer

ball

bake

moo

mud

Mike

knot

boo

bud

bike

dot

_____   _____   _____

Name   Date   Homework Partner

Nasalization Word Level

Busy Bear

Directions: Read/say aloud the picture-words below. Then, cut out the markers. Flip a coin (heads= 1, tails= 2) to determine how many spaces to move. As you move, read/say each picture-word aloud. First player to reach the finish wins.

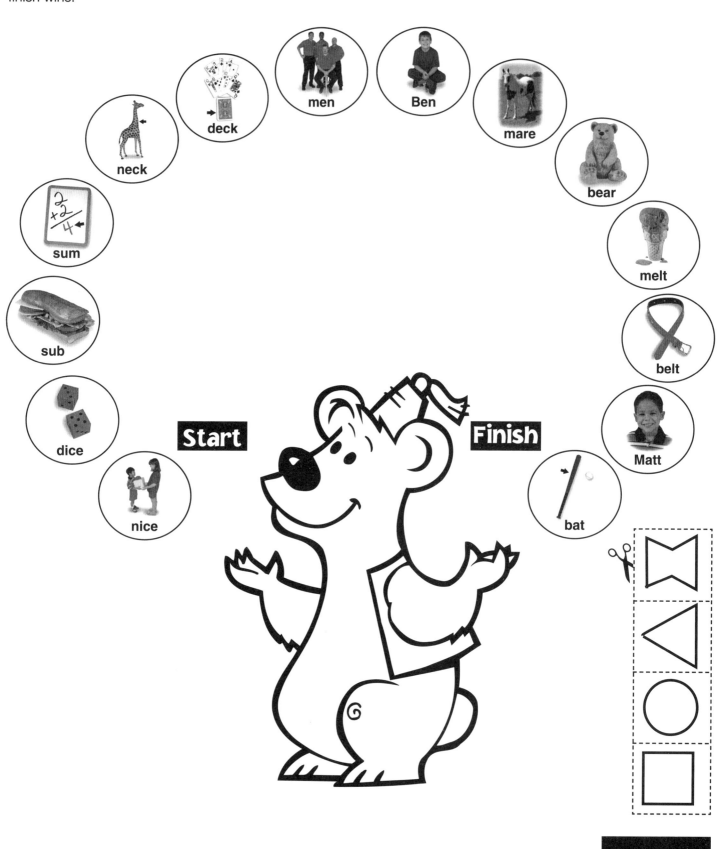

neck
deck
men
Ben
mare
bear
melt
belt
Matt
bat
Finish
Start
nice
dice
sub
sum

#BK-320 Webber® Photo Phonology Minimal Pair Cards Fun Sheets • ©2005 Super Duper® Publications • www.superduperinc.com • 1-800-277-8737

_____   _____   _____
Name   Date   Homework Partner

Nasalization Word Level

Sound Sorter

Directions: Read/say each picture-word aloud. Listen to the first sound in each word. Cross out the picture and/or pictures that do not start with the B sound. Then, read/say aloud only the words that begin with the B sound.

 **bug**	 **mug**	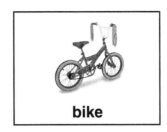 **bike**	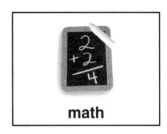 **math**
 **bake**	 **bath**	 **Mark**	 **bark**
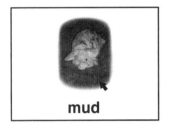 **mud**	 **bunny**	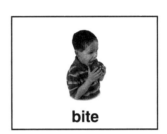 **bite**	 **moose**
 **money**	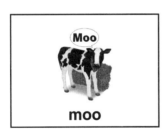 **moo**	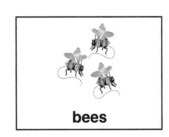 **bees**	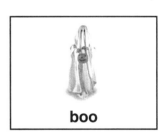 **boo**
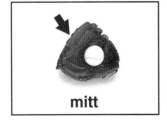 **mitt**	 **beg**	 **Meg**	 **beach**

_____   _____   _____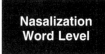
Name   Date   Homework Partner   **Nasalization Word Level**

#BK-320 Webber® Photo Phonology Minimal Pair Cards Fun Sheets • ©2005 Super Duper® Publications • www.superduperinc.com • 1-800-277-8737

Slide and Say

Directions: Read/say aloud the picture-words below. Then, cut out all the cards. "Slide" the cards down the slide, reading/saying each word aloud as you slide.

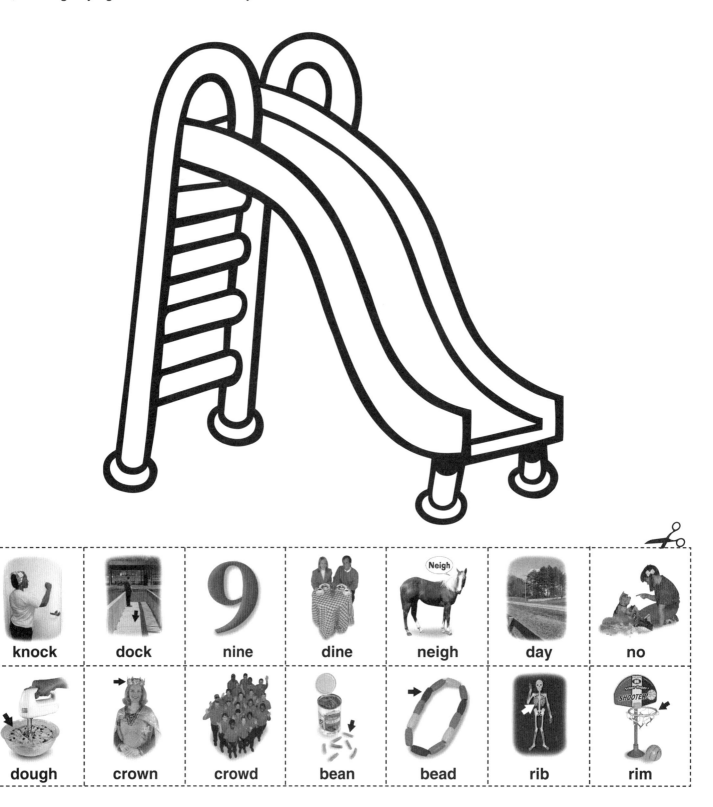

knock	dock	nine	dine	neigh	day	no
dough	crown	crowd	bean	bead	rib	rim

_____ _____ _____
Name　　　　　　　　　　　Date　　　　　　　Homework Partner

#BK-320 Webber® Photo Phonology Minimal Pair Cards Fun Sheets • ©2005 Super Duper® Publications • www.superduperinc.com • 1-800-277-8737

Complete a Phrase

Directions: Complete the phrases with the correct word using the Word Bank below. Read/say the phrases aloud. Variation: Roll a die to see how many times you have to say the phrases.

1. throwing the _____

2. _____ and ball

3. a _____ helmet

4. some cookie _____

5. a bubble _____

6. a yummy _____

7. rolling the _____

Word Bank

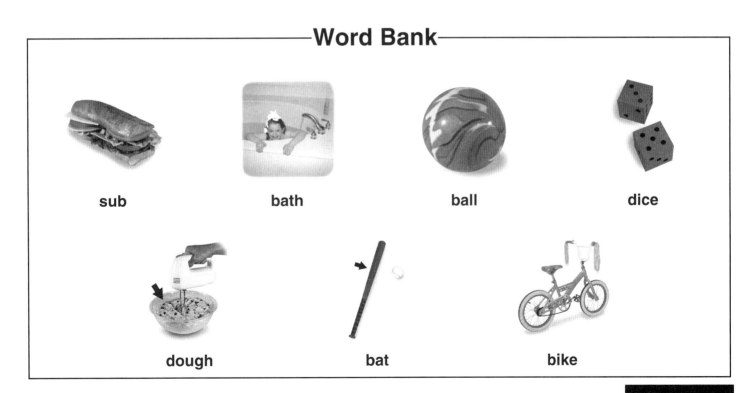

sub	**bath**	**ball**	**dice**

dough	**bat**	**bike**

Phrase Fill-In

Directions: Write a vowel in each blank space below to spell the words correctly. Then read/say each phrase aloud.

1. a d___ck of c___rds

2. a l___ather b___lt

3. a b___nny r___bbit

4. bo___t d___ck

5. b___g for a b___ne

6. a t___ddy b___ar

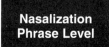

_____ _____ _____

Name   Date   Homework Partner

Nasalization Phrase Level

#BK-320 Webber® Photo Phonology Minimal Pair Cards Fun Sheets • ©2005 Super Duper® Publications • www.superduperinc.com • 1-800-277-8737

Puzzle Match

Directions: Draw a line from a puzzle piece in Column A to the one that matches it in Column B. Read/say the phrase aloud.

A

B

1. the loud

2. the crawling

3. a ride

4. a sunny

5. my friend

6. a polka

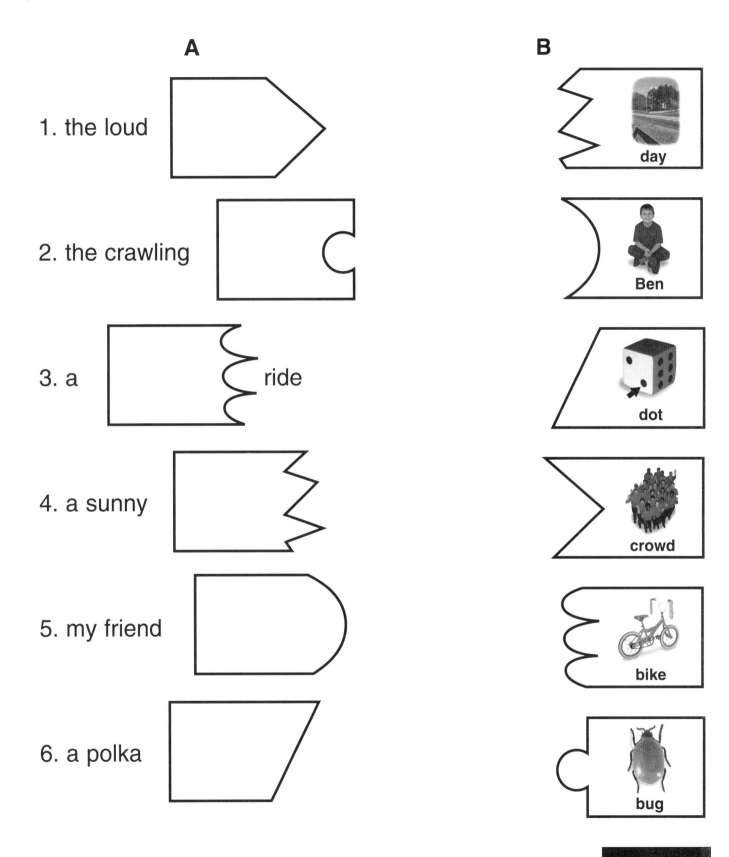

day

Ben

dot

crowd

bike

bug

Fix It! Phrases

Directions: Each phrase below has an underlined incorrect letter in it. Fix each phrase by saying/circling the correct letter on the right side of the book. Read/say aloud each correct phrase.

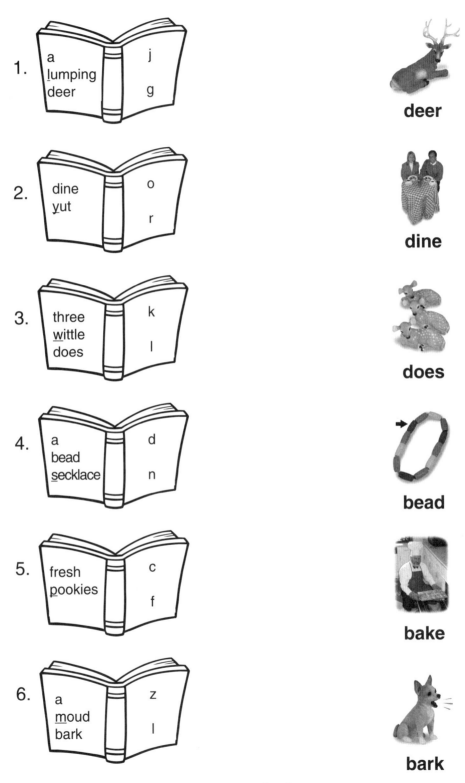

1. a <u>l</u>umping deer — j / g

2. <u>d</u>ine yut — o / r

3. three <u>w</u>ittle does — k / l

4. a bead <u>s</u>ecklace — d / n

5. fresh <u>p</u>ookies — c / f

6. a <u>m</u>oud bark — z / l

deer

dine

does

bead

bake

bark

Answer Key: 1. j 2. o 3. l 4. n 5. c 6. l

Nasalization Phrase Level

Name   Date   Homework Partner

"I would..."

Directions: Read/say the questions below. Answer them aloud, using the target word in a sentence.
Example: *"I would want my belt to fly."*

1. If you had a magic , what would it do?

   belt

2. If you planned a perfect , what would you do?

   day

3. If you found a , what would you teach it to do?

   bunny

4. If you got a new , where would you ride?

   bike

5. If you hit a home run, what would the do?

   crowd

6. If you could the world's largest cake, what would it look like?

   bake

7. If a could talk, what would it say?

   bear

_____   _____   _____

Name   Date   Homework Partner

Which One Fits?

Directions: Read/say each picture-word on the right. Then, complete each sentence by circling the correct answer. Read/say each answer aloud using a complete sentence.

1. Which one crawls?

    bug   **mare**

2. Which one blooms?

    neck   **bud**

3. Which one talks?

    meat   **Ben**

4. Which one bounces?

    ball   **mug**

5. Which one cleans?

    mud   **bath**

6. Which one is a noise?

    bark   **nine**

7. Which one is a vegetable?

    beet   **crown**

Answer Key: 1. bug 2. bud 3. Ben 4. ball 5. bath 6. bark 7. beet

Name   Date   Homework Partner

Nasalization Sentence Level

#BK-320 Webber® Photo Phonology Minimal Pair Cards Fun Sheets • ©2005 Super Duper® Publications • www.superduperinc.com • 1-800-277-8737

Toy Store

Directions: Read/say each picture-word on the shelves. Cut out the dollar bills below. Give a dollar bill to your homework partner as you pick out something to buy. Say, *"I want to buy (a) _____."*

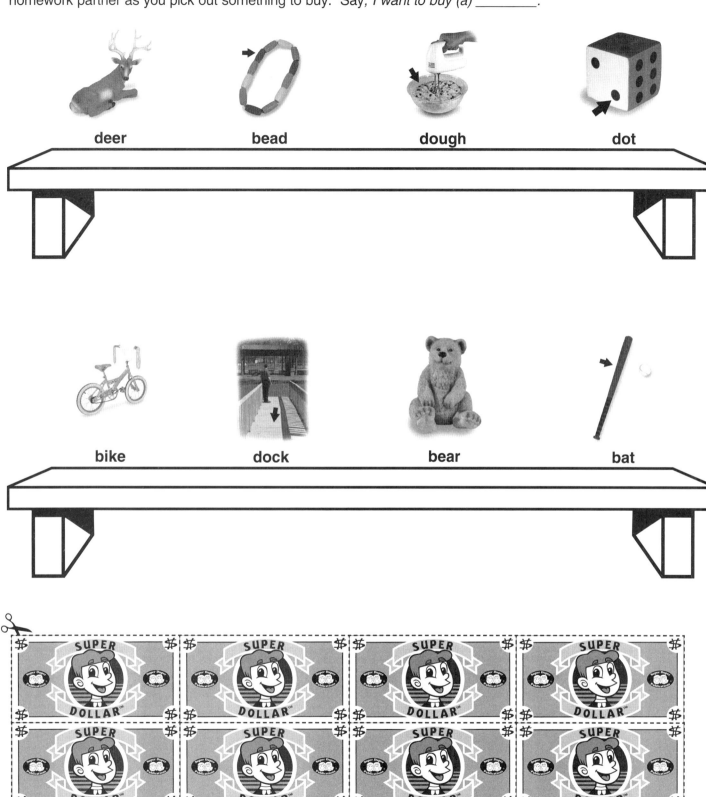

deer   bead   dough   dot

bike   dock   bear   bat

_____   _____   _____

Name   Date   Homework Partner

Scrambled Sentences

Directions: Unscramble each sentence and write it on the line below the egg. Then, read/say the sentence aloud.

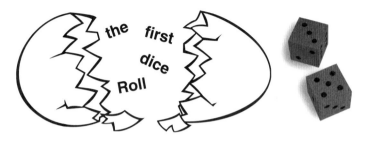

1. _____

_____ .

2. _____

_____ .

3. _____

_____ .

4. _____

_____ .

5. _____

_____ .

6. _____

_____ .

Answer Key:

1. Roll the dice first.
2. Let's dine out tonight.
3. Shuffle the deck before playing.
4. I want to ride my bike.
5. The ghost says boo.
6. Add the numbers to get the sum.

Aim for Good Speech

Presented to

_____

has improved his/her

production of _____ at the _____ level.
word/phrase/sentence

Awarded by _____ _____
Date

Shake, Rattle, and Roll

Presented to

_____

has great Phonology skills.

Awarded by

_____ Date _____

#BK-320 Webber® Photo Phonology Minimal Pair Cards Fun Sheets • ©2005 Super Duper® Publications • www.superduperinc.com • 1-800-277-8737

What's All The *Buzz About?*

Presented to

_____

has GREAT phonology skills!

Awarded by

_____

Date

Notes

#BK-320 Webber® Photo Phonology Minimal Pair Cards Fun Sheets • ©2005 Super Duper® Publications • www.superduperinc.com • 1-800-277-8737